PRETEND
WE'RE
DEAD

TANYA PEARSON

PRETEND WE'RE DEAD

The Rise, Fall, and Resurrection of Women in Rock in the '90s

GRAND
CENTRAL

New York   Boston

Grand Central Publishing
Hachette Book Group
1290 Avenue of the Americas
New York, NY 10104
grandcentralpublishing.com
@grandcentralpub

First Edition: January 2025

Grand Central Publishing is a division of Hachette Book Group, Inc. The Grand Central Publishing name and logo is a registered trademark of Hachette Book Group, Inc.

The publisher is not responsible for websites (or their content) that are not owned by the publisher.

The Hachette Speakers Bureau provides a wide range of authors for speaking events. To find out more, go to hachettespeakersbureau.com or email HachetteSpeakers@hbgusa.com.

Grand Central Publishing books may be purchased in bulk for business, educational, or promotional use. For information, please contact your local bookseller or the Hachette Book Group Special Markets Department at special.markets@hbgusa.com.

Print book interior design by Amy Quinn.

Library of Congress Control Number: 2024946757

ISBNs: 9780306833373 (hardcover), 9780306833397 (ebook)

Printed in the United States of America

LSC-C

Printing 1, 2024

This book is dedicated to the artists who shared their stories with me: Shirley Manson, Donita Sparks, Melissa Auf der Maur, Patty Schemel, Kate Schellenbach, Nina Gordon, Louise Post, Jill Emery, Liz Phair, Tanya Donelly, Tracy Bonham, Kristin Hersh, Lori Barbero, Zia McCabe, and Josephine Wiggs. Thank you for the music, for trusting me with this project, and for giving my life purpose.

CONTENTS

INTRODUCTION

GREW UP LISTENING TO POP AND TOP 40 RADIO. WHILE MY PAR-
ents lacked the intense musical curiosity I came to inhabit,
their tastes ran the gamut: Sade, Anita Baker, Luther Vandross,
Aretha Franklin, Guns N' Roses, the B-52s, Tears for Fears, the
Clash, Michael Jackson, the Tubes, and, of course, Madonna. I
thought that I was related to Kate Pierson. It didn't matter that
my last name was an adopted name and spelled with an *ea* rather
than an *ie*. They sounded the same, and we both had red hair. I
sang in the church choir and played alto saxophone. My mom
drove me into the city to watch jazz bands, and at the time, I
wanted to be a famous jazz saxophonist.

I was ten years old in 1991, the year "punk broke" and Nirvana altered mainstream music with their second album, *Nevermind*. Kurt Cobain was too much, too punk, for my delicate
sensibilities. It wasn't until 1994 that I listened to the album in
its entirety. Shortly after, I discovered Hole's *Live Through This*
and Sonic Youth's *Screaming Fields of Sonic Love*. I deemed their

greatest hits album "unlistenable," but "Death Valley '69" introduced me to '70s no wave progenitor Lydia Lunch. I convinced my mom to buy me a guitar and practice amp, followed by a drum set with one cymbal. By 1997, I started my first band and spent most of my free time in my basement room, which was plastered from floor to ceiling in posters and magazine covers, sneaking cigarettes, drinking warm Kahlúa, and writing songs on a digital eight-track recorder. I got a job at Compass Interactive Toy Store in the mall, not because I was interested in interactive toys but because it offered a paycheck and was in the same building as Strawberries record store and a Barnes & Noble. I didn't have a car, but sometimes my mom let me borrow her minivan. My half-hour, unpaid lunch breaks consisted of hitting up the bookstore, buying a *Rolling Stone* or *SPIN* magazine, speed-reading a Courtney Love article, discovering that she was greatly influenced by Kim Gordon, and then heading to Strawberries and ordering a Sonic Youth or Free Kitten album. At the time, MTV still played music videos late at night, and I'd lose sleep recording live performances on VHS tape to be reviewed and interpreted later. Rosie O'Donnell hosted a talk show (before she came out) and had musical guests like Veruca Salt. So did Jenny McCarthy (before she was an anti-vaxxer). I was too young to attend concerts on my own, but my mother was hip and attractive and brought my sister and me to clubs with crumpled copies of our birth certificates, demanding we be admitted with a guardian. That's how I was able to see Veruca Salt in person, as well as Garbage, Hole, Liz Phair, Letters to Cleo, Juliana Hatfield, and a smattering of male-fronted bands.

Women in rock of the 1990s were my archetype, and my main motivation was to be a drinking, smoking, drug-taking rock star. When I barely graduated high school in '99, I had mastered the first three activities. Only rock stardom eluded me. I was also aware of a strange shift in music. I didn't know what exactly had happened—and I was too drunk to investigate—but the "women in rock" wave had crashed, and the feminism of male allies like Kurt Cobain had begun to be replaced by overtly misogynist male rock stars, nu metal, teen pop stars, and boy bands.

I continued playing in bands with guys, at warehouse spaces in Providence, Rhode Island, during the experimental / noise music underground phenomenon. Thurston Moore and Kim Gordon even attended these shows in dilapidated buildings where smelly crust punks lived, worked, and performed. I sold plasma for beer money and recorded my own songs, shamelessly ripping off the Breeders, Sonic Youth, and Helium, in my shitty apartment and recruited friends to play shows. In the early 2000s, the White Stripes, the Strokes, and the Hives emerged from the underground to become the new alternative sensations on MTV. My friends began dressing like mods in black suits, white ties, and jet-black bowl cuts. They shaved their eyebrows and formed bands that sounded like the Rolling Stones, only not as good. Aside from Karen O and Peaches, nonconformist women in rock were nowhere to be found in the mainstream—and it's arguable whether Karen O is nonconformist or Peaches can be considered a mainstream artist.

After eight years of floundering around Providence and Boston; after eight years of being high, drunk, unemployable, and at times experiencing homelessness; and after a suicide attempt, intervention, and arrest, I checked myself into detox at age twenty-six. While my fellow "inmates" had friends and family members smuggle in drugs and mascara, I preferred CDs. Marianne Faithfull, Veruca Salt, Amy Winehouse, Cat Power, and Judy Garland became the soundtrack to my early recovery.

Therapists and counselors suggested I write, but all that came out were corny, depressing songs about sobriety. I resigned myself to the fact that being sober meant forfeiting creativity, wearing velour sweat suits, becoming heterosexual, dating a guy in a sober house, and listening to Eminem's *Recovery* album. In the mid-late 2000s, Nirvana, Pearl Jam, Alice in Chains, and the Foo Fighters were still played on alternative radio and classic-rock stations, but the women were still gone. Sheryl Crow survived by transitioning to adult contemporary; Gwen Stefani went pop.

I got sober and found work as a bagel-sandwich maker, dog walker, and video-store clerk, before eventually enrolling in community college. I was pleasantly surprised to find I wasn't a total moron. I did so well that I applied to Smith College and was accepted into their Ada Comstock Scholars Program for nontraditional students. As a former drunk and cokehead, I was decidedly nontraditional at this prestigious institution that claimed Gloria Steinem, Betty Friedan, and Sylvia Plath as distinguished alumnae.

During my first year, two things happened that changed the trajectory of my life: I got a job in the Smith archives and learned about oral history; and I wrote a paper about media representation using L7, the Breeders, and Veruca Salt as my main subjects. The problem was that I couldn't find enough primary source material to cite. I decided to interview them—and then I interviewed more women. And more! This was the birth of what I called the Women of Rock Oral History Project, and soon enough, I became the director of a national repository of video interviews, the exact primary source documents I couldn't cite when I was a freshman. And this drunk will soon hold a doctorate in history.

◎

As part of the Women of Rock Oral History Project, I have collected nearly seventy long-form video interviews to date, with narrators ranging from Viola Smith—one of the first professional female drummers in the United States—to Brenda Lee and members of Fanny; session musicians like Gail Ann Dorsey and Eva Gardner; punk and no wave progenitors Lydia Lunch, Alice Bag, and Exene Cervenka; '60s icons Melanie Safka and Marianne Faithfull; transgender and gender nonconforming artists Mz. Neon, JD Samson, and Lynn Breedlove; and many '90s rock women, including Shirley Manson, members of Hole and Team Dresch, Tanya Donelly, Kristin Hersh, Josephine Wiggs, Kate Schellenbach, Azalia Snail, Liz Phair, and Tracy Bonham. The archive continues to grow and is absolutely one of a kind. Following a self-guided format with a focus on the personal as well as the professional, the interviews cover standard topics like songwriting, recording, touring, the industry, musicianship, gear, and the creative process, but they start from childhood, with participants describing their upbringing, families of origin, education, personal relationships, parenting, and lives at present. They reflect on their contributions to rock history, their thoughts on gender, and women's place in rock music. After a few years of editing and transcribing, I noticed a recurring theme among the alt-rock women I revered as a teen.

In 2018, I interviewed Shirley Manson, iconic redhead and vocalist of the seminal '90s rock band Garbage. During the interview, she discussed her childhood, upbringing, and musical trajectory, but she also made a provocative statement: "It's a blanket fact that after September 11, nonconformist women were taken off the radio."[1] I wouldn't have put it in these terms, but what Manson said accorded directly to my own experience of listening to the radio and watching TV while I was a teenager and into my twenties. And if I had noticed something big in the zeitgeist through my haze of booze and tweaking, I figured there must really be something there. As I continued to interview more musicians who shared similar personal experiences (and horror stories), I began to suspect that the abrupt ending of their careers was less a matter of collateral damage and more a political instrument wielded in a new national-security state.

The 1990s had been a great decade for women in rock music. Hole, L7, Belly, the Breeders, PJ Harvey, Garbage, Luscious Jackson, Liz Phair, Elastica, Portishead, Sonic Youth, Veruca Salt, Alanis Morissette, and Throwing Muses made their way into public consciousness, while members of the underground riot grrrl movement found themselves deflecting media attention. Suddenly, nonconformist women were, if not everywhere, at least, and finally, out there. Old female archetypes—backup singer, chanteuse, folksy singer-songwriter, pop star—were complicated by frank lyrics, swaths of red lipstick, and feminist messages scrawled on bare midriffs in marker. Having been born and reared in a trailer park, I connected more with the blue-collar, working-class feminism of L7 and Hole. The riot grrrl movement lacked the artistic and aesthetic diversity of bands outside the liberal arts genre—riot grrrl bands did look and sound very similar—and as a high school student, anything representing a club or a clique ignited a fight-or-flight response. That is one reason you will not see riot grrrl represented in this book. It simply wasn't my cup of tea, and the movement eschewed mainstream recuperation. Riot grrrls actively denied the media access to their scene. They were not signed to major labels, and I do not consider Bikini Kill, Bratmobile, or Heavens to Betsy (for example) mainstream alternative rock artists. The third and final reason is that the riot grrrls have done an excellent job documenting their history; they've done such a good job that any loud, alternative rock women are labeled *riot grrrl* retrospectively.

By the turn of the century, women in the music industry who had been chart-topping successes found themselves shunned from rock radio. Retaliatory efforts were made: Sarah McLachlan initiated the traveling festival Lilith Fair in 1997, but it, too, was a victim of backlash and ended in 1999.[2] As I did with riot grrrl, I am mentioning Lilith Fair to acknowledge that other forms of musical feminism existed during this era, but I consider the separatist, kumbaya, singer-songwriter genre and the artistry and feminisms of the alternative rock genre as disparate and deserving of individual attention. Although her attitude has changed, Shirley Manson declined an invitation to perform at Lilith Fair, and L7 flew a banner over the festival that read, "Bored? Tired? Try L7." To be fair, the band flew one over the Warped Tour, too, that said, "Warped Needs More Beaver."

In the aftermath of the 9/11 terrorist attacks, and the ensuing war on terror, the United States reverted to the Cold War mythology of the protective male and dependent female. John Wayne and the damsel in distress. In her book *The Terror Dream*, Susan Faludi investigates the disappearance of women in the media—commentators, scholars, news anchors, and editorialists—but this disappearance extended to musicians, artists, and entertainers as well. There was no room for rebellious, feminist women; domestic femininity was used to repurpose and commodify the subversive messages of alternative culture and turn them into something more profitable like the Spice Girls (Girl Power!) and Avril Lavigne's skater boi corporate pop punk schtick. The 2000s marked the rise of hypersexualized yet arguably autonomous female pop stars like Britney Spears and Christina Aguilera, nondescript boy bands like NSYNC and the Backstreet Boys, and a wave of predominantly male indie rock. By 2002, bands like Hole and Garbage were no more.

What happened was a rolling back of the proverbial red carpet that had been laid out for this new era of alt-rock women. The death of Kurt Cobain marked an end of mainstream feminist men. By 1997, frat-boy nu metal rose to prominence on rock radio and MTV, and Woodstock '99 marked the end of a generation. The Telecommunications Act of 1996 allowed corporations to buy up as many radio stations as they wanted in a single market. College radio stations, women-centered stations, and Black radio stations were the primary victims of this piece of legislation. The creation of corporate media behemoths like Clear Channel coincided with the rise of nu metal, and women who had been chart-topping successes could no longer get airplay. Record labels also experienced massive consolidation during this time. Representatives were fired; bands were moved from one label to another without their consent and found that they weren't being supported and their records were being shelved. Finally, there was vocal backlash against third-wave feminism in the press; the most poignant example is *Time* magazine's 1998 cover story "Is Feminism Dead?" This cultural anti-feminism precipitated an anti-feminist agenda that emerged in mainstream media after 9/11.

Pretend We're Dead will examine the emergence and disappearance of women in rock in the 1990s and the ideological, attitudinal, and technological forces that allowed them to break into the mainstream but also bolstered their abrupt removal. This book will be a radical-feminist approach to understanding a historical moment, rooted in the past, that can help us better understand the mechanisms of control—ideological, psychic, and systemic—that continue to subjugate women in rock. I'm relying heavily on Susan Faludi's *Backlash* and *The Terror Dream*, and Silvia

Federici's *Caliban and the Witch*, and this book will be deeply anchored in the lived experiences of women in rock, told in their voices, and supported by my work as a former drug-addict-turned-scholar and avid fan writing for a trade audience. I'm not interested in the sex, drugs, rock and roll narratives, and I'm not interested in accepting women as an inherently marginalized group of creators working in a male-dominated industry. Instead, I hope to present a new understanding of the alt-rock phenomenon in the 1990s, as well as the cultural climate from which it emerged.

THE INDUSTRY LANDSCAPE HAD BEEN LARGELY CONSERVATIVE IN the 1980s—conservative in the sense that women were relegated to pop categories and primarily visible as video vixens and sexual objects. The corporate music industry had extended into television (MTV), film, and mainstream print magazines. Grunge music was a reaction to this, the pretense and showmanship of pop and hair metal, the failure of Reagan-era "trickle down" economics, and the dismantling of the welfare state that left a new generation of youth disenfranchised, unemployed, and frustrated. The feminist ethos of '70s punk and its egalitarian, participatory nature reemerged at the end of the '80s and early '90s, when the subcultural grunge movement became a mainstream, global phenomenon with the release of Nirvana's *Nevermind*. College radio and independent record labels provided new avenues for underground artists to reach wider audiences and acted as a bridge between subculture and the mainstream. Women benefited from these new platforms and the inclusivity of grunge. Major-label representatives also benefited from these platforms and capitalized on the opportunity to discover the next Nirvana. They descended on indie scenes like sharks with a scent for blood and a briefcase full of money, signing any band with potential, leading to a mass exodus of bands from independent labels to the majors.

While mainstream media has a history of appropriating subcultural trends, what was most unusual about the 1990s was how diverse rock music—and popular music in general—was. Despite attempts to retrospectively categorize the phenomenon as "grunge" and male dominated, women were active participants, and their catalogs ran the gamut. It remains a golden age in music, and an era of artistic, creative control before the massive consolidation of media, production, and record labels. The '90s saw an explosion of forms of femininity, a mash-up of genres, and cross-pollination of sounds and influences. The power of college radio and MTV cannot be overstated: they elevated nonconformist women to mainstream rock stardom in a way we had never witnessed in this country and have not seen again. And they did so in many guises, which itself is one of the most remarkable qualities of this unprecedented, understudied, and revolutionary time. The media had a difficult time corralling and categorizing the feminisms of '90s rock women, and history has had a similar problem.

I blame my aversion to performative justice on having come of age during a time when alt-rock women were inherently political and inherently feminist without branding themselves. Female-fronted bands in the 1990s were opinionated, vitriolic, and actively engaged in various political campaigns and social justice initiatives. Rock for Choice was a series of benefit concerts founded by L7 and the Feminist Majority Foundation, lasting from 1991 to 2001. The band performed at the Los Angeles Gulf War protest rally in 1991. In 1992, Bikini Kill performed outside the Capitol Building at an event protesting the Supreme Court's antiabortion stance.

Women in rock in the 1990s were socially conscious, storytellers, aware of gendered embodiment. Because they emerged from such diverse backgrounds geographically and socioeconomically, and because their influences were so broad, the music and lyrical stylings were multitudinous. Indie and alternative rock today is constrained by corporate overlords, social media culture, and an infatuation with the self and personal identity. Consequently, lyrical navel-gazing is the norm, and everyone kind of looks and sounds alike. Part of what made the '90s so unique is the breadth and diversity of the artists within the genre, but also the breadth, diversity, and nuance of its feminism as it emerged in the music and in performance.

Pretend We're Dead is a history book, but it is also inspirational and relevant to our present in a number of ways (previous examples included). After fifty years, a largely conservative Supreme Court overturned *Roe v. Wade*. We're in the wake of a global pandemic and political division and are inundated with images of disenfranchised Americans retaliating against racism, corporate overlords, sexism, homophobia, transphobia, and police brutality, via a consolidated and partisan news media. The #MeToo movement held Hollywood and political bigwigs like Harvey Weinstein and Jeffrey Epstein accountable for sexual assault and trafficking before moving into the music industry and local music communities. Subsequently, "cancel culture" is rampant, for better or worse—but that's another book. Presently, mainstream music is a homogenized product, a direct result of media and record-label consolidation that began in the mid-1990s. Pop music presently follows a distinct pattern, is produced by a handful of people, and generally sounds the same.

A lot of '90s rock women continued to make music, tour, and create, but mainstream media is ageist, youth-obsessed, and sex-obsessed, so they weren't granted access to audiences after their bloom of youth faded.

What's left of the music industry has found new ways to exploit musicians' labor. In 2022, many artists called for a boycott of the music streaming app Spotify. Oddly enough, the protest was heralded by older generations—from Neil Young, Joni Mitchell, and David Crosby to India Arie and members of Belly (the band's profile banner read, "Delete Spotify"). The real chart-toppers who could truly make a difference—the Taylor Swifts, the Miley Cyruses, the Dua Lipas—haven't gone anywhere. Not that there is anywhere to go, at this point. And even when artists want to leave Spotify, the musicians themselves have little say and rarely own their catalogs or publishing rights. The decision is left with the Big Three—Universal Music, Sony Music, and Warner Music—who have licensing deals with Spotify (so do the few remaining indies through music-rights agencies). Belly can protest, but they must go through their labels to get their songs off the platform. In the late 1990s, streaming emerged as an alternative to major-label exploitation and indentured servitude. Major labels have figured out how to get their grubby paws in the digital realm and make shitloads of money while continuing to exploit artists.

Women of Rock Oral History Project narrators describe the downfall of their careers as a backlash and the result of various factors. Feminist backlash itself has been well documented by historians and journalists like Susan Faludi, Jennifer Baumgardner, Amy Richards, and Ruth Rosen—Rosen's book *The World Split Open* includes a time line of the modern women's movement with signs of backlash in heavier type—but women rock musicians have yet to be considered (1) feminist, political actors and (2) casualties of backlash. This book will present backlash as part of a historically rooted continuum, and it will break down the mechanisms that disappeared women from the mainstream, taking seriously the claims and experiences of women who lived through it. While artists like Shirley Manson blame conservative post-9/11 culture, Kate Schellenbach, Liz Phair, and Tracy Bonham note the effects of nu metal misogyny and record-label consolidation as the culprit. Tanya Donelly recalls a meeting with her label (Sire Records), who informed her that there were just too many women on the radio at the time, in 1995. And Nina Gordon and Louise Post, co–front women of Veruca Salt, describe four years of sexualization in the media, belittlement by male musicians, and parasitic management that pitted them against each other, insisting there could be only one lead singer.

Chapters 1–3 will explore the rise of women in rock. These chapters utilize the oral testimony of Women of Rock Oral History Project narrators describing who they were, where they came from, their experiences as working musicians in underground music scenes; how college radio and independent record labels acted as publicity machines before widespread use of the internet and social media; and how the advent of the egalitarian and feminist grunge phenomenon changed the musical landscape, igniting a major-label feeding frenzy, allowing women in rock to emerge in the mainstream as a powerful, highly visible, cultural force. Chapter 4 examines what happened at the apex, including major-label record deals, music festivals, touring schedules, the recording process, and music video production. Chapter 5 illustrates the overt and assorted feminisms and political activism inherent in music and performance during this decade.

Chapters 6–9 break down the multiple components that composed the backlash, explaining the phenomenological, political, and systemic causes of women's disappearance from mainstream media: from the public reaction to the death of Kurt Cobain and thirty-year vilification of his wife, Courtney Love, to the rise of nu metal and the symbolism of Woodstock '99, to the corporatization of the music industry, the rise of Clear Channel, its ties to the Bush administration, and finally the anti-feminist, nationalist sentiment after 9/11. Chapter 10 considers the sea change that emerged in mainstream rock radio in the early aughts. Some women maintained their careers by shifting to pop or adult contemporary while others went on indefinite hiatus. The Epilogue explores the 1990s resurgence as it has emerged in anniversary tours, reunions, new albums, and documentary films.

This book will avoid the tendency to synopsize women in rock and will go beyond surveying their roles as artists and creators. It will present a new understanding of the rock phenomenon in the 1990s, as well as the cultural climate from which it emerged. My goal is to think about women in rock outside (but not apart from) the confines of rock history and to place them in the broader context of feminist, political, and social history. Rock music is an important historical category; it reflects the politics and culture in which it is produced and, as I hope to illustrate here, influences politics and culture.

My main intention is to take women's claims seriously—to investigate the rock phenomenon in the 1990s and to explain what might have contributed to their complete disappearance from the mainstream by the early aughts. Other writers, journalists, and scholars have written about gender, the media, and September 11, the history of feminism and subsequent backlashes (Susan Faludi, Noam Chomsky, Silvia Federici); they have published oral histories of subcultural, antiestablishment scenes (Legs McNeil and Gillian McCain), rock encyclopedias (Lillian Roxon), and oral histories of women in rock (Maria Raha, Lucy O'Brien, and Helen Reddington, among others). In 2019, Jessica Hopper, Sasha Geffen, and Jenn Pelly published "Building a Mystery: An Oral History of Lilith Fair" in *Vanity Fair* magazine. At the end of the piece, artists refer to a Lilith Fair backlash and cite the rise of boy bands and female pop stars as the culprit. While pop certainly usurped rock in the early 2000s, it was more a consequence of broader anti-women, anti-feminist sentiment rather than the singular causal factor. But this article is perhaps more closely related to my topic than any book.

No one has seriously looked at women in rock in the 1990s as agents of political change—specifically, nonconformist women as instigating the return of normative gender roles after 9/11, in a new national-security state. We certainly weren't going to see Courtney Love on the cover of *Rolling Stone* after a terrorist attack on US soil. As a matter of fact, Love may have launched the "crisis in masculinity," which left the country vulnerable to such an attack. Maybe this sounds conspiratorial, but editorialists and political pundits perpetuate this idea, especially during times of war or national crisis. Love was a loud, outspoken feminist and drug-taking rock star. An unfit mother (as she was described in the press) and a widow accused of killing her husband, who just so happened to be the voice of a generation. Love, in a tattered dress, lipstick smeared, wielding a signature Fender guitar (my sister owned one; I had the Kurt Cobain signature Mustang), screaming into a microphone with one leg resting on a monitor so you could almost see her vagina—she was the kind of feminist woman who wouldn't wear underwear. This rock and roll archetype had no place in mainstream media after 9/11, as it was the antithesis of the Cold War femininity promoted in male-dominated—and freshly concentrated—media.

September 11 revealed an ambiguous, undiagnosed facet running deep in the American psyche resulting in the denigration of women and magnification of "manly" men.[3] Women in media disappeared within days of the attack. Male political pundits, editorialists, and journalists blamed feminism for "soft" men and believed that the new climate of danger would quell the "anti-male agitation we've endured for so long." The post-9/11 press disenfranchised and disappeared feminist writers, but it was barely noticed while it was happening. And this is perhaps the most important aspect of anti-feminist backlash as it has occurred throughout history, and in this case, as it has affected women in rock. Just because it isn't glaringly obvious doesn't mean it's not happening.

Pretend We're Dead argues for the radical potential of rock-music history that is focused on feminist issues. By presenting a historical narrative that is aware of the distant past, attentive to continuities over time, and alert to the workings of patriarchal power, it invites readers to reconsider the struggles of the twenty-first century.

PART ONE

Chapter 1

FAST AND FRIGHTENING

Some people may say, "Oh my God, you're so arrogant for even saying that," but we were hot shit in the underground.

—Donita Sparks, L7

IN 1991, I WAS CROWNED MISS PRETEEN BOSTON. I WAS NEW TO the pageant circuit (sadly, it was my first and last pageant), and I'm pretty sure I beat the more seasoned contestants because I could answer the emcee's questions, like "If you could be anyone other than yourself, who would you be, and why?" articulately, without crying. I was not a particularly attractive child. I was ten years old, and my favorite artists were Debbie Gibson and Madonna. For the evening-wear portion of the event, I wore a knee-length, gold party dress and white, fingerless lace gloves, à la Madonna Louise Ciccone circa 1985.[1] Unbeknownst to me, Sonic Youth released a documentary that year, crowning 1991 "the Year Punk Broke." The film follows the band on a tour of European festivals with supporting acts Dinosaur Jr., Gumball, Babes in Toyland, Mudhoney, and a then unknown Nirvana, capturing a special subcultural moment before the impending cultural (grunge) revolution. I bought the movie on VHS in 1997 and immediately regretted being born in 1981. In hindsight, I think I came of age at the perfect time. Too many rock historians and journalists demand that you "had to be there" in order to comment on long-gone rock scenes. But I was tragically uncool, a very late bloomer, the oldest child with no hip older siblings to steal records from. As a matter of fact, I didn't know what the fuck vinyl was until my late teens, and I didn't start purchasing records until my early twenties. Now I'm the irritating aunt who makes my niece and nephew wait while I sift through bargain bins at flea markets.

Because I was too young to go to concerts until the mid-1990s, I depended on the mainstream media that, by the early '90s, created space and visibility for alt-rock, nonconformist women in magazines, on television, and on the radio. I could watch Sonic Youth perform on *Late Night with David Letterman*, hear Hole and L7 on my local radio station, and spend money on mainstream magazines with the purpose of butchering them and covering my bedroom with glossy photos of Juliana Hatfield, Kim Deal, Nina Gordon and Louise Post, Courtney Love, Melissa Auf der Maur, and Patty Schemel. The only man in my bedroom was Kurt Cobain. So yeah, I wasn't there, at the basement shows or at some small club in the middle of nowhere watching L7 before they made it big. But I was a part of the countercultural, global phenomenon that reached its peak in the mid-'90s, as a young fan, and therefore, a living, breathing testament to the importance of mainstream visibility. Had these women not been embraced by rock radio and MTV, I might have missed it entirely.

In 1994, I asked my mom to buy me an electric guitar and began stealing cigarettes out of the vending machine at Bickford's Family Restaurant. Bickford's was directly across the street (a busy highway) from the Hanover Mall, where I spent most of my free time and allowance money on CDs. This was the year I discovered rock music—not just rock music, but female-fronted rock music. I have a visceral memory of unwrapping Hole's *Live Through This* CD, obsessing over the artwork and liner notes, and hearing the first song, "Violet," pumping through the speakers of my boom box. I can't say that I liked it, but it obviously influenced my impressionable, virginal mind. Almost overnight, I hid my Madonna tapes and embraced a new generation of feminist women. I had no idea where they came from, what this new genre was or how it evolved, and I didn't have much interest in its point of origin. What I had was an insatiable appetite for the music and any information about the women who made it. This was pre–household internet. No Google, no iPhones, no computers. I did analog detective work in real time, harassing sullen, dowdy bookstore employees with questions they were not equipped to answer; they looked sad when I ordered Poppy Z. Brite's Courtney Love biography, and a confusingly pornographic novel called *Sexing the Cherry* (because Louise Post recommended it in a *SPIN* magazine interview) in which penises were referred to as "members." There were a lot of swollen members in that book.

Eventually, I bought a little TV/VCR combo and stayed up way too late recording music videos. MTV actually played music back then, and 120 *Minutes* was like the cable TV version of college radio, featuring underground, emerging artists. College radio was also a thing—a big thing. There were alternative rock stations, too, but college radio played up-and-coming artists who would (inevitably) get signed. When I was nineteen, closeted, fully imbibed with alcohol, and in love with my best friend (it's unfortunate, but it happens), I had a threesome with her and some allegedly cool guy who had a radio show at Brown University. We met at the station and played some songs, he told me I had a voice for radio, and apparently, that was grounds for my first real sexual encounter. That's how cool college radio was.

At sixteen, I started my first band, Thriftshop Apocalypse. I wanted an all-girl band but couldn't find a drummer in my art class, and so my friend Chris was recruited. I figured it was fine because Hole had Eric Erlandson. I'm sure everyone's first band isn't that great—we were terrible—but enough time has passed that I find it endearing, not embarrassing. We played one show under a gazebo in a park with two all-male bands; one was ska, the other metal. I loved Hole, L7, and Liz Phair, but I wanted to infuse harmony and the pop sensibility of Veruca Salt, who were my absolute idols. I even wrote a song called "Veruca Salt" about meeting them after their concert in Providence, Rhode Island, in 1997. Louise still has our demo tape, which I meticulously decorated with black roses and thorns—I'm sure I had a lot going on, emotionally, at sixteen. When my family bought a computer, I found girls from around the country in chat rooms who liked the same music and played in bands. We sent one another mixtapes, fanzine clippings, and magazine articles in the mail and forged pen pal relationships that probably would not have happened were it not for this unprecedented moment in the history of rock music. I had always loved music. I had always had a soundtrack, but I had never seen myself represented—and on such a grand scale—in mainstream music before the grunge revolution.

The categories of rock and alternative music were redefined in the 1990s by the advent of grunge, a genre of rock music that emerged out of Seattle in the mid-'80s. There is some dispute over who originally coined the term: it's been attributed to Mark Arm of the band Mudhoney, Bruce Pavitt of Sub Pop has taken credit, and finally, Everett True, a UK journalist visiting Seattle to document Sub Pop bands subsequently popularized the term. More important than who said it first is the sound, as it emerged in the late '80s, characterized by heavy, distorted guitar, and elements of both punk (Flipper, the Germs, X), classic rock (Led Zeppelin, the Beatles, and Heart), and metal (Black Sabbath, Judas Priest). Bands like Green River, The Melvins, and Mudhoney were progenitors of grunge, while Nirvana, Pearl Jam, and Alice in Chains were some of the most commercially successful (and widely remembered) of the grunge movement—interestingly, these bands sound nothing alike. But in the late '80s, "grunge" did define a specific sound that had a lot to do with location, production, and promotion. Sub Pop had become *the* label, and famed engineer Jack Endino recorded Soundgarden, Mudhoney, Green River, Nirvana, Blood Circus, Hole, L7, the Gits, and 7 Year Bitch, among others. In 1991, Nirvana's *Nevermind*, Pearl Jam's *Ten*, and Soundgarden's *Badmotorfinger* were all released. With three alternative stars hailing from the same region, mainstream music media adopted the grunge label to describe this new Seattle sound. Despite the sonic diversity, any band from Seattle was lumped under the moniker, and by the mid-'90s, any rock bands playing electric guitars and wearing flannel shirts or ripped jeans were categorized as grunge as well.

The historical memory of grunge has reinscribed what was an explicitly anti-sexist, gender-neutral movement as inherently masculine and male dominated. This revisionist history elevates men, singles out spokespeople (Kathleen Hanna, Kim Gordon, Courtney Love), and forgets everyone else or has retrospectively relabeled them riot grrrls. Compartmentalization has been a useful tool in defusing threats to patriarchal systems, and the rock industry is a patriarchal system that reflects broader patriarchal culture. Women in rock in the 1990s were central creators in dozens of regional scenes across the country and to the global phenomenon that usurped pop and even knocked Michael Jackson out of his #1 slot on the Billboard Hot 100 chart. They emerged as equal players and became an influential force in the mainstream in the early to mid-'90s by way of democratic, egalitarian scenes that were heavily influenced by the inclusivity of punk. Women actively engaged as performers and surfaced as members of and contributors to their respective scenes across the country.

While grunge blossomed in Seattle, the riot grrrl movement began in the early 1990s, when a group of women at Evergreen State College in Olympia, Washington, held a meeting to discuss how to address sexism in the punk scene. Riot grrrl encouraged active engagement in cultural production, and girls started bands and created their own music and fanzines. The bands associated with riot grrrl—Bikini Kill, Bratmobile, and Heavens to Betsy—used their music to express feminist viewpoints and wrote deeply personal songs that dealt with topics such as rape, incest, eating disorders, and misogyny. The grunge phenomenon revitalized rock and alternative categories, and after the release of *Nevermind* in 1991, industry representatives descended on Seattle, Boston, Los Angeles, and other major cities in search of the next Nirvana. Before the term *alternative rock* became common usage around 1990, the music to which it refers was known by a variety of terms, such as *indie, punk,* and *shoegaze,* and *college rock* was used in the United States to describe alternative music outside the mainstream that flourished via college radio during the 1980s. To understand how nonconformist, feminist rock women became a mainstream cultural phenomenon, it is important to understand where they came from, socially, culturally, economically, and geographically.

TANYA DONELLY AND KRISTIN HERSH FORMED THEIR FIRST BAND, Throwing Muses, when they were teenagers, in Newport, Rhode Island. I grew up in Rhode Island, and I can attest to something that Kristin says: there isn't much to do there except maybe go to the beach or start a band. There was a flourishing hardcore scene on the East Coast and Throwing Muses created a space for themselves in it, playing weird, sometimes disturbing, indie pop that both confused and delighted audiences. They were played heavily on college radio—like the Rhode Island School of Design (RISD) and Brown, performed at parties and college campuses, and found companionship and kindred spirits (and eventually 4AD labelmates) in the equally as weird, Boston-based band the Pixies.

Tanya Donelly (Throwing Muses / the Breeders / Belly): Jim, Kristin's dad, gave me a guitar, and my dad gave her one. I don't know how it worked out that way, but we ended up with each other's father's guitars. They both played. My dad was mainly just singing [Bob] Dylan songs around the house. Her dad wrote his own songs. And that was sort of our songwriting camp, going to his house and playing his songs with him and then learning Beatles songs and Dylan songs, and then writing our own stuff almost immediately on the back of that.

My parents were divorced by the time I was seven, which is also when I met Kristin [Hersh]. Newport is very small, and our families became close. And then that sort of segued into a relationship between our parents—my dad married Kristin's mom. I think the foundation of this sort of survivable chaos sort of gave us both the vulnerability and the strength to be in a band. There was this feeling of anything that we do that's going to be scary is still going to be okay, and we had each other. People often say, "It's so brave that at fifteen you started doing what you were doing," but compared to what we were coming from, it felt extremely measured and extremely safe and well thought out and logical and sensible.

Kristin Hersh (Throwing Muses / 50 Foot Wave): I started the band when I was fourteen, and we just played what anybody else would have played. We wrote songs, but they were not alive, and it was fun, but it was not a passion, because I had sort of lost my passion when I learned the rules. I got hit by a car and started to see songs as colors—what came back to me was very passionate, but it was also very obsessive and terrifying. No one wants to hear music that no one else hears. And it was not continuous. When a song needed to happen, it would grow in volume, and when I learned it, which was just listening, it would fade, and then I wouldn't be haunted by it anymore. But I had to serve the songs. And I'm not real kooky or groovy. I was a biology major. I wanted everything to make sense, and this didn't, and so I guess you'd call that a love-hate relationship. Or a love-terror relationship with music, which lasted for many, many years.

We lived on Aquidneck Island in Rhode Island, a place that is very grim and also very beautiful. There's not a lot to do, so you either surf or play in a band, and none of us could surf, so that's kind of why we had a band. I taught my sister, Tanya, to play guitar, and our drummer, Dave, had been my best friend since I was eight years old. It was a way to get invited to parties that we wouldn't have been invited to. But then after my accident, it got kind of nutty, and we were still playing parties. We thought, *We're a band. We should play exciting songs now.* We had lots of friend fans, and we made demos and played them in their cars, and it was just sort of a little community. We played on hardcore bills and in clubs. We were still in high school, and we would drive to sound check wherever it was, somewhere in New England or in New York, play whenever they told us to play, even if it's seven o'clock and nobody's there, and then load out at three, and you drive home and get up for high school.

JILL EMERY IS A VISUAL ARTIST AND BASS PLAYER FROM SOUTHERN California. She befriended a fellow punk, Rozz Williams of Christian Death, as a young teen and frequented Los Angeles clubs in the late 1970s and early '80s. Emery was part of the first incarnation of Hole and played bass on their first album, *Pretty on the Inside*, before joining Mazzy Star in the mid-'90s.

Jill Emery (Super Heroines / Hole / Mazzy Star): I was born in Montebello, California, but grew up in Diamond Bar, California. My parents split up when I was fourteen. I have two brothers, I'm in the middle, so there's Eric, me, and then Mark. My mother worked for doctors. Back then, I swear I was like, "Mom, this sounds like you guys were the Wild, Wild West."

She was in urgent care, she did a little schooling for this, but she was taking X-rays, giving shots, drawing blood. The doctor's like, "Hold this while I'm doing surgery." I just couldn't believe it. I would say, "How much are you getting paid?" as I got a little older, and I swear it felt like a little above minimum wage. Honestly, she just did whatever she could to keep us afloat, and she was amazing. I don't know how she did it. I guess she scrimped a lot. We had a nice house in the suburbs, so we were safe in that situation.

I got into music, and I was the offbeat one in the family, I guess they call that a black sheep, in every way. Being gay—and the only girl in an Italian family—that's harsh in that situation. Being vegetarian at the time, everything was just like, "God, everything about you," and being a musician, throwing that in. I would go into LA, and I would meet women at the punk shows. I would date them, if you can call it that at fifteen. I was very nervous because I knew my mom was not going to be thrilled. She had expectations: "Meet a guy, get married, have kids." Thankfully, my brothers fulfilled that. They've got great kids, and my mom's the greatest grandma. That being said, it took a while, even though it was obvious.

I moved in with my grandma when I was seventeen because there was turbulence with my mom at the time. However, when I started my first punk band at fifteen and a half, I couldn't really play that well, but my mom would let us rehearse in the garage. We were called the Asexuals, and it was Rozz Williams and I— he was Roger at the time, and he went on to do Christian Death and Shadow Project. We met in high school, and we were just two little punkers. I saw him in a Ramones shirt, and I was wearing a Runaways shirt that I made; we didn't have any money. My mom was cool. She let us rehearse songs called "Slow Death" and "You're So Plastic" and "Mannequin Depression"—that was pretty cool, shockingly.

I was painting at the time, too, but it was more expressive, and I wasn't taking it that seriously. I was lucky, at age fifteen, everything at that time was really blossoming, in the sense that my suburban world was opening up. Somehow, I met Art De Leon, and he had a building. Who could have a building? How do you have that? I guess he rented a space in Pomona, which was ten minutes away from my house, and he would let us put on art shows. We would make films on his Super 8 cameras. He was just open and said, "Let's do this. Let's just do whatever we want." I think Christian Death played there. A lot of punk bands came through there and played. It was a dive, and it was always being busted.

Olivia Rodrigo said she was massively influenced by Babes in Toyland during the writing and recording of her album *GUTS*.[2] Drummer Lori Barbero cofounded Babes in 1987 with her friends Kat Bjelland and Michelle Leon in Minneapolis, Minnesota.

Lori Barbero (Babes in Toyland): I was born in Minneapolis, Minnesota, and lived there until my dad got a job in New York City, and then my family moved to Pearl River, New York, in Rockland County, just a few miles from the George Washington Bridge. You could see New York City from my bedroom. My mother didn't necessarily encourage music as a career, but she loved music. We always had a giant stereo console, those big, huge things, in the living room. And she always had music playing all day every day, kind of like what I do. But it was like Roberta Flack, the 5th Dimension, Barbra Streisand. And my dad's mother really, really loved music, too. She gave me my first album, which was a Chicago double album, and I still have it. I got that when I was in grade school, so I probably got it the year it came out. She had one of those, you pay a penny, and you get this record, like Columbia House. The Jackson 5 was my first concert, and I had the Jackson 5 album. I was in sixth grade and went to that concert in the Twin Cities.

My grandma really loved Black artists. So I got a lot of her records: Billie Holiday and Joan Armatrading, and all the old Ray Charles and just all the really cool old stuff.

I played piano for maybe two days, and then I played the violin for maybe one day. The drums were really my first instrument. And I started at the age of twenty-seven.

I just always went to concerts even when I was young. Then I started going to New York City, and everyone in the small town I was in just could not believe that I'd go to New York City. They were freaked out. They just thought I was just insanely crazy. But I went there all the time. I was like fifteen, sixteen, seventeen years old, going to see Queen and David Bowie and Pink Floyd and Suicide, and Patti Smith and Bruce Springsteen. I went to Rockland Community College and saw the Marshall Tucker Band and the Charlie Daniels Band, and I liked all of that stuff. I went to everything from Marshall Tucker to the New York Dolls.

ACCORDING TO COURTNEY LOVE, PATTY SCHEMEL IS "HER DRUM-mer." And she is the longest-lasting and most memorable drummer of Hole, who just so happened to join the band during the writing of their second album, *Live Through This*, an album that remains one of the most important albums of the decade—and, I would argue, the twentieth century. Schemel grew up in the small, working-class town of Marysville, Washington. She was gay, a tomboy, and found refuge behind the drums, and camaraderie in the local punk scene.

Patty Schemel (Hole / Upset): I grew up in Marysville, Washington, a small town north of Seattle. I was in a band called the Milkbones in the early '80s. We were in high school, and there were two guys at my school who were also into punk rock. Once I discovered punk, I felt at home because there were freaks like me in punk. And I saw more women playing punk rock music than I did playing rock music on MTV. I started writing songs and playing drums in the Milkbones, and we played at our high school and at parties, and that's how it began. There was a big punk rock party at a barn up at the middle of nowhere, and back then, we would draw maps to the location. All these punk rockers showed up to this little country barn and we played, and then afterwards, we networked with the other bands. It was always after playing those shows, a friend would say, "So-and-So's band needs a drummer," and, "They saw you play at this party and want to know if you want to play," and then it just goes from there. Being a good drummer was such an esteem builder, and it became my entire identity. I was Patty Schemel, the drummer.

MELISSA AUF DER MAUR WAS HOLE'S THIRD BASSIST AND JOINED the band after Kristen Pfaff died tragically of a drug overdose. She grew up in Canada, the daughter of eccentric, anticapitalist parents, and was encouraged to pursue music, art, and photography. She played in local bands and befriended Billy Corgan (Smashing Pumpkins) who introduced her to Courtney Love.

Melissa Auf der Maur (Hole / Smashing Pumpkins / Auf der Maur): My parents were epic independent, freewheeling, choose-your-own-adventure types. They were both freelancers for their entire lives. My mother, Linda Gaboriau, was 100 percent first-wave feminist. She ended up in the grand world of Quebec theater, via her own radio show and broadcasting. She went from journalism to theater and became the leading literary translator. Her passion is to bring the French-Canadian theater voice to the rest of the world. My dad, Nick Auf der Maur, took his journalism into radio and then a remarkable television show that he had from '69 through '72. Both my parents fought for the underdog, for the French. My father ended up becoming a politician and running on and off in downtown Montreal for twenty years. He has a street named after him, and when he died, his funeral was the biggest funeral in Montreal history.

JOSEPHINE WIGGS'S ROCK MUSIC CAREER BEGAN WHEN SHE CHOSE an electric guitar over a pet parrot. She has continued to choose music over everything else, ever since. Born in a small town outside London, England, Wiggs was an eccentric kid with eccentric parents, and she idolized Siouxsie Sioux. She joined the Breeders during the writing of their first record, *Pod*, and wrote the infamous, instantly recognizable bass line that made "Cannonball" the band's biggest hit.

Josephine Wiggs (the Breeders / Ladies Who Lunch / Dusty Trails): I grew up in a town called Letchworth [England]. It was the first garden city, and it was a planned community built on the principle of having the best parts of living in a town and the best parts of living in the countryside. And it was all very much built on kind of humanist and possibly Quaker principles. There were no pubs. It's mentioned by George Orwell in— I think it's in *The Road to Wigan Pier*, and he makes fun of it.

My mother was a schoolteacher. There weren't a lot of career options when she was growing up. She was born in 1931, and pretty much being a teacher was one of the few things that was open to her as a professional woman. She said, much later in life, that she would've quite liked to have become a solicitor, which is a lawyer. My father also trained as a teacher, probably because he couldn't think of anything else to do! He studied art and geology at college, and then he became a primary school teacher. He didn't do it for very long, maybe a couple of years, because although he liked the children, he couldn't stand the structure and the rules. So he quit his job and stayed at home and looked after us when we were very little so that my mum could keep her job. He was one of the first stay-at-home dads, basically.

It was a creative household. My father was very creative, very willing to do things with us. I vividly remember the day, the last day before I had to go to school at the age of five, and he and I built model airplanes out of two pieces of wood that we nailed together, painted with watercolor, and hung up in the trees. He was always willing to spend time doing things like that, certainly with me. I think because I'm the youngest.

I started taking cello lessons when I was six. And this was partly because we happened to have a cello. My parents had a lodger who left the cello behind. And then I became interested in it. And there was a lady that lived across the road from us whose name was Miss Farmes, with an *E*. And she was a music teacher. She was principally a piano teacher, but she also played the cello and taught the cello, and so I went and had lessons with her.

I was a little bit influenced by my elder sister's record collection. My elder sister, Sarah, who's five years older than me. I remember she had like *Station to Station*, David Bowie, and a Brian Eno record that I really liked. *Taking Tiger Mountain (by Strategy)*, I think it was. And get ready for this. People are very shocked and surprised, but I loved *Tapestry* by Carole King.

KATE SCHELLENBACH GREW UP IN NEW YORK CITY AND CAME OF age when the punk scene was alive and thriving. She lived in a loft with her mother and sister and learned how to play the drums on a set that a friend stored at her house (her mother agreed to the arrangement on the condition that Kate could use them). At twelve, she formed the Young Aborigines, an experimental hardcore band with Mike Diamond. They recruited Adam Yauch, Adam Horovitz, and became the Beastie Boys, and transitioned fully to hip-hop. Schellenbach was soon fired and went on to drum for the Lunachicks before joining Luscious Jackson.

Kate Schellenbach (Beastie Boys / Luscious Jackson / Lunachicks / Ladies Who Lunch): I grew up in the West Village in Manhattan, New York City. My parents were together until I was about eight, and then they split up. I continued to live with my mom, and we grew up mostly in the Village. There was a year in Brooklyn, and then a good part of my life was in a loft on Fourteenth Street in Manhattan, which was cool. My mom and dad played a lot of classical music. My mom was into Laura Nyro and Labelle and Peggy Lee and vocal music. The Beatles were big, and I think that's when I first got interested in music. Then I started going to camp and going away from home and meeting people who were listening to the B-52s, the Clash, and Blondie. That's when I became obsessed with music.

DONITA SPARKS—L7'S SINGER, GUITARIST, AND LEGENDARY tampon-thrower—grew up in Chicago and moved to Los Angeles after high school. Her father was a high school principal, and her mother was a feminist who went back to work when Sparks was eight. She was the youngest of three daughters and watched in horror as her cool older sisters "toed the line," going to college and working minimum-wage jobs. She worked as a foot messenger in high school and saved up to move to Los Angeles without a plan or an agenda.

Donita Sparks (L7): I grew up on the south side of Chicago— very middle class. I knew I wanted to get out from a young age. I saw my sisters graduate college and get stuck working dead-end jobs. I knew I wanted to be a performer, but I didn't have an idea about what that looked like.

I knew I wanted to move to LA very early on. Probably even before I heard the Ramones, like when Bowie was in Berlin and stuff, and I was in seventh grade. I wanted to get the hell out of the south side of Chicago. And it was either move to the north side of Chicago or move to Europe or move to New York. And then one day after clubbing, I was probably sixteen, I was with my friend at Lake Michigan, and it was a beautiful night, and the wind was blowing off the lake, and I was like, "God, it's so beautiful! Where is it like this all the time?" And he said, "LA." I became obsessed with the idea of moving there. All I really knew about LA was surf music, and I thought I'd be a surfer. I didn't know the LA punk scene or anything like that. But after high school, I started working more to save money to move to LA. I think I ended up with about $1,200.

My sister's friend let me stay on her couch for a month until I found my own place in Hollywood. I started dating a guy who worked at the *LA Weekly*. He was the dispatch guy for all the messengers that would deliver the papers, and he got me a job doing that part-time. I was working at the Egyptian Theatre, literally popping popcorn, and making minimum wage on Hollywood Boulevard. And then I got that job at the *Weekly*. The art department liked me because I dressed wild and I was friendly, and I think they just got a kick out of me. I was nineteen, and they said, "Hey, do you want to work in the art department?" And I was like, "Yeah! Hell yeah! How do you do it?" I wasn't doing anything super artistic; it was just called the art department, production, or whatever. They taught me how to wax the stuff and lay it out and make sure it's straight with a T square.

ANOTHER CHICAGOAN, LIZ PHAIR, STARTED WRITING MUSIC UNDER the name Girly-Sound, in 1991. She made three extensive bedroom recordings, which, until 2018, were never commercially released, though they made the rounds among the underground tastemakers of Wicker Park. Looking back on them today, they fill out a picture of an artist who had a unique perspective, style, technique, and sound.

Liz Phair: I have always had a sense that music was important and valuable. My parents were both music lovers and would take us, when my brother and I were young, to various musical theater productions. And I think half the time that we went to church, we went to the choral arrangements, which my mother was fond of. She played piano and sang. There was a sense in our family that someone might get on it at any given moment at a family gathering, sing something, or that we would play music with every meal and enjoy summer concerts, whatever was appropriate for both parents. So I would say music was always really important to us as a family.

I had taken piano lessons most of my life, and I had taken guitar lessons, from eighth grade on, both classical and folk. So there was a sense in my family that creativity was always supposed to be a part of your life, but much less of a sense that you would ever do it professionally, which is an interesting dichotomy in this.

One of the things I think is interesting, looking back at my career and those of my peers, is the extent to which technology dictated what we ended up doing and what we became known for. I was not inclined toward technology at all, but I recorded songs to cassette on a four-track TASCAM from the '70s and '80s. It just seemed approachable. I could quietly, at home, record against myself vocally to do harmonies, backing vocals. And I could also layer the guitar part. I would just repeat the same part. And it turns out, I learned later, once I was doing this professionally, I'm very consistent when I write a guitar part. It's pretty much that part exactly every time. And as Keith Richards likes to say, "If you layer an acoustic guitar enough times, it becomes electric."

My four-track era was during my college years at Oberlin in Ohio and when I was living at home, going to the Art Institute of Chicago; I also did four-track recording when I was living in New York. I was interning for Nancy Spiro and Leon Golub, two married artists on the Lower East Side. I would just drag my TASCAM with me and my guitar everywhere I went. In New York,

I had my electric guitar, but not my acoustic. And I would just have to, very quietly, in the back room, because I had to share an apartment with two other girls, record my electric, acoustically, on multiple tracks so it would even be audible.

NINA GORDON AND LOUISE POST ARE CO-FRONT WOMEN OF THE alternative rock band Veruca Salt. Their predestined, cosmic collaboration started well before they met. Both grew up middle-class children of well-educated parents, and both experienced the divorce of their parents at a young age. Music was a comfort, and they were weaned on musicals and folk songs and began singing as children. Neither seriously considered pursuing music until college, and both were majorly influenced by seeing female-fronted bands like the Breeders, L7, and Wendy & Lisa.

Nina Gordon (Veruca Salt): I grew up moving around quite a bit—Washington, DC; Boston; Madison, Wisconsin; New York; Chicago—and my parents were hippies. I was born in 1967, and my father was a law student. He was teaching law in Madison and was part of many demonstrations. We lived there at a university in 1969/70, so it was a volatile time. My parents were super into music. We grew up with great music—a lot of Beatles, Bob Dylan, Jimi Hendrix, Stones—and there was always music in our house. My father played guitar, my mother sang and played piano, and music just figured heavily into everything we did. It was not the most stable upbringing—like I said, we moved around a lot, and my parents' relationship was sort of rocky from the beginning, so music also played a super-important role in my emotional life, making me feel safe or, you know, comforting myself, and the same was true for my brother, who is also very musical and is also in the band with us. But my parents separated, got back together, things were always kind of shaky.

Louise Post (Veruca Salt): I was born in 1966 in St. Louis [Missouri] in a hospital which is no more. I had an older brother and sister and a younger brother, and like Nina, my parents were on rocky soil for most of my childhood and they split up when I was eight. They met in a summer choir in St. Louis, and so music was a big part of their relationship. And then they were both singers, and they both sang with me from a really young age. My mom played guitar, and we would sing at family parties. She taught me how to sing harmony, and that was the best thing ever. It was the best thing even as a small child; we would sing things like "Yellow Bird" and "Four Strong Winds," these sort of classic folk songs, and it was so much fun, and it's a really nice memory I have.

SHIRLEY MANSON REACHED THE HEIGHTS OF ALT-ROCK CELEBRITY as the—at times—"overexposed" (her words) front person of 1990s supergroup Garbage. But Shirley Manson's success predated her Garbage days. Manson joined the Scottish band Goodbye Mr. Mackenzie when she was nineteen and even toured with Blondie in the 1980s before forming her second band, Angelfish. Garbage drummer Butch Vig was a successful producer, having recorded Nirvana, Smashing Pumpkins, and Sonic Youth. He saw Angelfish on MTV's 120 *Minutes* and sought out the ginger goddess with a contralto vocal range to audition for his new band.

Shirley Manson (Garbage): Music was something for fun in my household. It wasn't considered a career in any way, shape, or form. And I certainly wasn't overly encouraged by my parents. I just had a natural inclination towards music. My dad wanted me to go to university—that was what he was interested in. I had a more academic sort of upbringing in some ways than I did a creative one. I didn't even know what creativity was until much later in my life. I mean, I'm talking like into my late thirties, early forties. I didn't really understand what being a creative was. I know that sounds weird, but I came from a really straight upbringing. My parents got along, they didn't argue, I didn't see anything weird. My mom wore an apron and warmed our pajamas on the stove in the morning.

I grew up in Edinburgh, Scotland. I was the '60s baby raised into the '70s by my parents. My father was a university professor. My mum was essentially a housewife, a term that's thankfully gone by the wayside. I have two sisters—I am the middle child, and that has had a massive bearing on my personality. We were essentially a middle-class family. My parents were really loving, I got along with my sisters, went to a great school. My high school had a separate music department and recording studio, and I benefited from that. My mum was an amateur singer and sang with a local swing band called the Squadronaires. Music was a huge part of our growing up. My mom used to play records, and I played in the school orchestra, sang in a choir, and I was selected by my school to study violin, piano, and clarinet, so I had a full musical upbringing.

TRACY BONHAM GREW UP IN THE PACIFIC NORTHWEST AND DIDN'T consider fronting a rock band until college. She grew up singing and is a classically trained violinist—an instrument that featured heavily on her 1997 debut album *The Burdens of Being Upright.*

Tracy Bonham: When I was little, I saw my mom onstage. She happened to be the lead in the musical *On a Clear Day You Can See Forever*. She was quite good, and I knew I wanted to do that. I helped her with her lines and her dance moves at age five. And I just thought like, *This is my bag*. I was born in Eugene, Oregon, and my mother was a singer. And then she became a music educator, and my father was a journalist, and he became an editor of the newspaper. My father passed away before I was two years old. My mom was a single mom for a while, and she also had three children from a previous marriage, so she was dealing with a lot. Because my siblings were so much older than me, I had to fend for myself and be the one that cheered everyone up or stayed out of the way. The reason I'm saying this is because it shaped my personality in so many ways, and it's why I started to write songs later in my life, at age twenty. I didn't know how to communicate with people, especially if it meant confrontation. My songs became very cathartic in how to say something that's uncomfortable to someone.

Singing was my first passion, but I didn't really study it. It just came naturally. I would say that violin was my first instrument where I got serious about it. I was also taking piano lessons, and that was fun. It was a great foundation, but I think violin was like my first real committed endeavor.

Jill Emery: We would play the clubs, but the funny part about that band is it was really fun. I think we put out one single, and the way the scene is, Ed Culver did the cover, and he did all the bands. He's amazing. And if you look at his archives, he was there documenting it. It was great. But anyways, so we somehow headlined in Orange County over Social Distortion. Now, I don't know how. We were just like, "Oh yeah, Social Distortion with those fake English accents," but I ended up really liking them. You're just dumb and you're a kid saying things and pretending you're in a gang. I don't know.

So, we're headlining over Social Distortion. Then, in the meantime, our first show out of town is in San Francisco and we're opening for the Dead Kennedys, and I don't even know how any of this happened because I kind of was in Daydream Land, even though I wasn't doing drugs or drinking, I was very daydreamy. After the Super Heroines, I was doing just tons of odd jobs, making jewelry in this loft in LA. I lived in LA at the time, and it was all women in there, all girls, so it was crazy. But Laurel Stearns said to me, "Hey, this band is looking for a bass player. Are you interested?" So, I thought, *Oh, okay, I'll check it out.*

I went to the rehearsal studio—I can't remember where we were, in LA, I guess—and it was Hole. And I go in there and the energy was just crazy. I mean, Caroline [Rue] was there, Eric and Courtney, and I go in and I'm trying to understand their songs, but there was something about it that I related to. It was very turbulent, though. Why would I relate to turbulence? I don't know. But, well, probably stuff going on inside of me that I didn't express. But as I was leaving, I didn't really say anything. I just kind of left after I said, "Okay, well, talk to you guys later." And then Courtney comes out and corners me at my car and says, "Well, you want to do this, right? You're going to be in the band, right?" I'm like, "Well, okay. Yeah. Sure. Let's do it."

We would rehearse at Jabberjaw, another club at the time, and we would play shows. But honestly, it felt like six people in the audience and one of them was my partner, Stacy, at the time. She witnessed everything, but basically no one was in the audience. And then all of a sudden, as time went on, it started growing. Courtney was very good at getting us press. It started with

Flip Side, and then I can remember one little thing, and it seems funny, but people can relate to it, I'm sure. She got Roddy Bottum from Faith No More to wear our Hole T-shirt in their video. It was like, "Okay, I understand how this works. We're going to do this; we're going to do that." I was like, "Okay, great. Good. Go for it. You're doing good."

Josephine Wiggs: My first band was called Attack of the Puppet People, which was named after a really dreadful film. My friend Floyd named the band. He was my sister's boyfriend at the time. He was a really good guitar player, so, after the cello, my next instrument was electric guitar. I pestered my father to get an electric guitar. On Saturday mornings, we would go into town, and on one side of the road, there was a pet shop, and they had a parrot in a cage in the pet shop. So I would go and look at the parrot and, like, try and commune with the parrot and look at it and think what an interesting thing it was and how I would like to have one. And then after I'd done that, I would cross the road to a store—it was really kind of a home electronics store—and they happened to have an electric guitar for sale. So I would look at the parrot and think, *God, I really want a parrot*. And then I would cross the road and look at the electric guitar, and I would think, *Oh, I really want an electric guitar*. And my dad said, "You can't have both. You've got to choose." And so, at the time, I chose the electric guitar.

It was such a piece of shit, to use a technical term. It was really hard to play and it didn't sound very good, and I did not get on with it very well at all. And then my sister's boyfriend said one day, "You should get a bass guitar, because then we can play together." So that's what I did. I made my dad buy me a bass guitar. And then we formed a band, which was Attack of the Puppet People.

I was a huge fan of Siouxsie and the Banshees and saw her a bunch of times. Gang of Four. I did see Sonic Youth play at University of London Union in the early '80s, or mid-'80s maybe it was by then? And Kim Gordon made a big impression on me. And Kim Deal, of course. I saw the Pixies. Strangely enough, when I saw the Pixies, I was like, "Oh my God, this is so weird. They're so goofy."

Shirley Manson: I was in my first band, Goodbye Mr. Mackenzie, for about ten years. I joined in 1984 when I was nineteen. We were signed to Capitol Records, EMI, and then we got grabbed by Radioactive Records, which was headed up by Gary Kurfirst, who was a very well-known music manager at the time. He saw us open for Blondie in the 1980s and signed us immediately. We went to Berlin to make a record, spent the entire $100,000 advance on drugs and alcohol, and came back to Edinburgh with nothing to show for it, at which point he dropped us. But he held on to me because he believed in me. He was like, "I just think that you could end up doing something."

After that, I took the role of lead singer in Goodbye Mr. Mackenzie, and the lead singer of the band became the lead guitarist. We just sort of jiggled things around and got re-signed as Angelfish. It caused a lot of tension between me and my bandmates because suddenly, I was being asked questions by the record label, and I was making decisions.

Lori Barbero: I went to college for two quarters at the University of Minnesota in Duluth (UMD), but I couldn't do it. So, I went to the cities, and worked at a punk rock club where every band played: the Clash, Iggy Pop, the Replacements, Suicide, Blondie. Hüsker Dü always played there, but they weren't really punk rock at all.

That's where I kind of got exposed to all that. I was probably twenty years old, and I started working there at maybe nineteen? I went to Key West, Florida, after I graduated, and then I went back up to the cities because my parents moved back. So I worked at the punk rock club, and from there on out, it was just music was my whole life.

I started a record label called Spanish Fly, I managed bands, and I booked tours. I had done that whole aspect of rock and roll and gone to every concert in the world. Every band that came through Minneapolis stayed at my house. The only thing I hadn't done was play in a band. And then I met Kat [Bjelland] in '85, and then we started getting together in '87. And then that's when Babes in Toyland started, I guess, from what Wikipedia says. I don't really know our history that well. Recently, someone asked, "When did you start?" And I'm like, "I don't know. Late '80s." And my friend said, "Nineteen eighty-seven. It's in Wikipedia." So now I just say '87.

Patty Schemel: I left Marysville and moved to Seattle intent on being a musician. I got a job at Microsoft and went to a lot of shows. I would go to this warehouse job every day and come home and play shows and go to my other job doing telephone installations, which was pretty lax. I was playing drums in an all-girl band, Doll Squad, and in Sybil with my brother, Larry.

Seattle wasn't a hot spot at that time. It wasn't like LA, New York; it wasn't a place for bands to stop on tour. It was a small scene before Sub Pop began. I met Bruce Pavitt, who started Sub Pop, and he showed me the Green River record, the band that splintered off and became Pearl Jam and Mudhoney. He talked about his idea for what Sub Pop will be, and at that point, he had a Sub Pop compilation, and he did a thing at the Vogue Club called Sub Pop Sunday, which was a goal for me in bands.

I met Kurt [Cobain] from playing shows. And Dylan Carlson, Slim Moon, Calvin Johnson, and all the people from Olympia. They had a different thing happening there—a kind of naive artist simplicity, and I really liked what Heather Lewis was doing in Beat Happening and what Bikini Kill were doing. There were a lot of trips to Olympia to see bands play, and I met Kurt that way, through that scene, and then I moved to San Francisco when I was in Sybil.

THE BEASTIE BOYS ARE REMEMBERED AS A LEGENDARY ALL-MALE, all-white hip-hop group from New York, but Kate Schellenbach met Adam Yauch, Mike Diamond, and Adam Horovitz when they were teenagers, attending shows and sneaking beers. At the time, the guys had a band called the Young Aborigines and invited Kate to play percussion because she looked punk and was inspired by the Slits. The Young Aborigines became the original hardcore/punk incarnation of the Beastie Boys. When Schellenbach was seventeen, the Beastie Boys recorded a proto-rap track called "Cooky Puss." The song was a hit on college radio in major cities like New York, Boston, and Detroit. Fledgling producer, DJ, and frat-boy-turned Buddhist Rick Rubin offered to DJ for the band, and together, they put together a rap set. Soon after, Kate was released from her duties, the Beastie Boys got famous, and Rubin got rich as founder of Def Jam Recordings.

Kate Schellenbach: I started going to see live shows when I was thirteen or fourteen. The first band I ever went to see live was the Student Teachers at CBGB. They were a great young punk pop band. In fact, I had gone to school with the drummer, Laura

Davis. For me, it was this perfect storm of seeing women playing live and being personally connected to them.

I met the guys in the Beastie Boys when I was fourteen. We were in a band before the Beasties called the Young Aborigines, which morphed into the Beastie Boys. I was in the band until I was about seventeen. The last music I did with them was a proto rap thing called "Cooky Puss," which was very weird. It was a prank phone call laid over a disco beat. We were still doing punk music, but still playing this new stuff and trying to figure out how to do it live. "Cooky Puss" was getting played on college radio in New York, Boston, and Detroit, and people wanted us to play shows. The boys met Rick Rubin, who at the time was a just a kid who went to NYU, and he offered to be our DJ. Rick was starting Def Jam out of his college dorm room, and we transitioned more to rap. We'd still play our punk stuff, but we put together a rap set.

Rick would DJ, and we all wrote raps. I think I only performed with them, this way, three or four times, and it was not for me. The boys were good at it, but I wasn't. I liked being behind the scenes, playing drums. I didn't want to be a front person. Rick convinced the guys that they had a future as the first white rap group. But he didn't like me, he didn't like girls rapping, and he didn't want me to be involved. I was about seventeen, and they informed me that they were going to go with Rick, without me, but we could still play music together under a different name. That happened for a while. I was playing punk music with the Beasties under a different name while they continued making their rap music, which became *Licensed to Ill*.

Donita Sparks: My first band was called the Debbies. And I did that on a dare. A woman who worked at the *LA Weekly* who was a drummer, a punk rocker, heard I played guitar, and she said, "Come on, what are you afraid of? What are you afraid of? Come on down." I'm like, "You know what, I don't have an amp, I'm not good enough." And she's like, "Well, you've got to be better than Suzi Gardner." We wore housecoats and curlers and played Venus covers. It was just this all-female, silly shtick. After that, I started a band with the art department of *LA Weekly* called the Shrews. I think we wanted to be the B-52s. And that was just fun party rock, but there were some feminist lyrics in there, too.

The scene in the LA '80s was very jumbled. There were people doing performance art rock like the Shrews, there was heavy metal, the Silver Lake bohemian scene, cowpunk, hardcore. It wasn't a solid scene, but we all played at the same clubs. I got to know who Suzi was, because she was dating my ex-boyfriend, who had gotten me the job with *LA Weekly*. And she was working at the *Weekly*. I was in the Shrews, and I wanted to play something harder, and I was sick of fucking around. I went over to Suzi's apartment in Silver Lake, her tiny little studio, and she played me a cassette of some stuff that she was working on, and I was like, "Oh my God, this is exactly what I want to be playing. This is exactly the kind of shit I want to play," which was a little bit Stooges, a little bit Motörhead, a little sludgy—it was hard rock without being metal. And that's really kind of what I wanted to do. And nobody was really doing that at the time.

We didn't intend to form an all-girl band, and one early member was a guy. After that, we decided we wanted to be all-female because he would get drunk, call us bitches, had trouble with authority, and he refused to play at a gay bar. He was a nice guy when he was sober, and very helpful, and kind of macho in a cool way, you know, like, "Oh, let me carry that for you." Before that, we didn't care. But at the time, it was a situation of the kind of rock music we wanted to play. Dudes who wanted to play that kind of rock didn't want to play with chicks; that's what I gathered out of our experience. And chicks were not that into playing what we were playing. We were in a bit of a predicament there. Suzi and I really struggled—we were playing with a bunch of people who were, you know, I would say at times unstable, and it was really depressing and kind of dark.

Kristin Hersh: Throwing Muses got great reviews because frustrated journalists were bored, and we didn't bore them. I suppose we were women, but that hadn't occurred to us. It was really that there was this indie scene, and then suddenly we were called *alternative*. I'm not sure it was ever even used before. We were insulted. Anyway, they started saying that I was crazy and that this was an alternative to anything else, and that was our hype, which we took to be sort of negative. We didn't really get it, but it was still hype, so we were packing clubs and eventually headlining, and then eventually, we were courted by almost every major [label], and we just kept sitting down in their fancy restaurants where they took us and saying, "What are you thinking? No one is going to like this! We don't even like it!"

We were the first American band to sign with 4AD. It was a one-record deal, and if we wanted to stay after that first record, we could. We recorded in this high-end studio in Massachusetts. He sent a high-strung British producer over who kept getting electric shocks. Everything he touched shocked him, so all he did was scream. I was by then about eight months pregnant, and we were almost finished recording when Deep Purple, the old fart band, decided that they wanted to be in this studio, and they kicked us out. But my first baby, Dylan, was born when that record came out in 1986. We released two EPs in '87, *House Tornado* in '88, *Hunkpapa* in '89, and *The Real Ramona* in 1990.

IN THE EARLY 1990S, INDEPENDENT RECORD LABELS SUPPORTED A patchwork of burgeoning regional scenes in major cities across the United States. Throwing Muses were signed to the European label 4AD after self-releasing their first cassette in 1985; no wave New Yorkers Sonic Youth released their first two albums on SST, a Long Beach, California, label focused on punk and heavy metal; LA scenester Jennifer Finch joined L7, and the band released their self-titled debut on Epitaph Records in 1988 before moving to Sub Pop in 1990; Hole released *Pretty on the Inside* on Caroline Records in 1991; Babes in Toyland hailed from Minneapolis and signed with their hometown label Twin/Tone. Minty Fresh—a Chicago-based label founded in 1993—launched Veruca Salt's career, released the Cardigans' first US album, and the debut single, "Carnivore," by Liz Phair. In terms of the grunge/alternative phenomenon that would take over mainstream music in 1991, Sub Pop is the best example of an independent label manufacturing (and exploiting) its own sound and creating a regional brand identity. In terms of women in rock, independent labels offered tour support and publicity. By the mid-'90s, hard-rocking women were highly visible and inspired the next generation to start their own bands.

Melissa Auf der Maur: I started working in bars way too young, at like fifteen years old. I was a ticket girl at the big punk rock club where everyone played. I saw Nirvana, Sonic Youth, the Melvins, Helmet, and I saw Hole open for Buffalo Tom in front of fifteen people, right before *Pretty on the Inside* came out in 1991.

I saw the Breeders and L7, too—so there were a bunch of women that I got exposed to, and they gave me the notion of like, "Oh, I can do that, too."

My father bought me my first bass when I was seventeen, and I tried out for an all-girl band. It was a weird, uptight rehearsal, and my impression was they were preparing their band name and their logo before they even knew how to play an instrument. That was this weird moment in my life where I understood that I didn't want to join a girl band. I really wanted to learn how to play music. And what ended up happening was all the guys that deejayed at the bar were those girls' boyfriends, and they all played in huge, established, indie rock, punk rock bands in Montreal. So I started my first band, Tinker, with them. The big joke is our eighth show ever was opening for Smashing Pumpkins during the *Siamese Dream* tour because I wrote a letter to Billy Corgan.

Lori Barbero: We played in my basement and rehearsed all the time. All the time. I swear, five days a week, sometimes seven days a week. It was just so fun getting together with Kat. There were two other members at first, but they weren't around very long. I think we did one or two shows with them. We were a four-piece when we started, and the singer wasn't in the band anymore. Then we got Michelle Leon, and then we were a three-piece, and Kat played guitar and sang. That's how that happened.

We were considered pretty weird when we first started playing shows. There were a couple of female bands in Minneapolis, but they were not in your face. We were very aggressive; melodic, but really loud, and we wrote all our own songs, and we just weren't afraid of just being like, "What you see is what you get." We were really heavy and abrasive from the get-go.

We played locally for a couple of years, we didn't really do much, but then in 1991, we went to Europe with Sonic Youth, and then after that, because Sonic Youth was already so established, that's when we went back to the cities and played with them in the main room. And then after that, we didn't play for free and we were respected, and we became established. We worked really, really hard, but they broke us.

Louise Post: I started writing songs in college, and I did some open mics. I would put off homework to write music. I mean, it was just the greatest excuse to not do anything. I did audition for a band in college. That was hilarious. I answered an ad in the [*Village*] *Voice*, and I went down somewhere around Forty-Second Street—which already sounds great—and there was a guy who played the guitar, a real preppy white guy who played guitar with two strings like the B-52s guitar player.

Tracy Bonham: After two years of conservatory-type schooling at USC, I decided to go to Boston. I had a friend at Berklee [College of Music] already, and I went to visit and to see what it was like. It seemed easier, and Berklee at the time was not as hard to get into. That was the beginning of a tough time in my life. And that's what I wrote my first album about. I was just about twenty, I was on my own, I moved from the West Coast to East Coast, three thousand miles away from home instead of one thousand miles away. Boston was completely foreign to me.

I was in Boston in the late '80s, early '90s. Before I discovered Nirvana, all I knew about rock music was the hair bands, and I didn't like that. I didn't like the melodies of any of those rock bands and hair bands. I hadn't discovered the Pixies yet or any of those cool Boston-based bands. When Nirvana came along in

1991, it totally opened my eyes to melody and rocking distorted guitars. That's when I thought, *Hey, I might want to start a band.* The furthest I could see in my imagination, though, was a popular band in Boston. I didn't expect to get a record contract or tour the world.

Kate Schellenbach: It was a big bummer getting kicked out of the Beastie Boys. Basically, they became huge. I was kind of turned off from music for a while. It wasn't until after college that I came back around and got interested in playing in bands again. The band that made me excited again was the Lunachicks. I played drums with them for a while—maybe 1990, '91? I realized there was this through line of good humor and music. It really works for me. The Beastie Boys were kind of a comedy band, and the Lunachicks were sort of a comedy band, but incredible musicians and badass. I got to know those girls and then played with them for a tour. Around the same time, I reconnected with Jill [Cunniff] and Gabby [Glaser], who are the main songwriters in Luscious Jackson.

Jill and Gabby had been living in San Francisco and made a demo tape. They gave their demo tape to Mike Diamond of the Beastie Boys to get notes. At the time, the Beasties were just thinking about starting their own record label. They really like this demo and offered to put it out on Grand Royal. Then they decided to put a band together. That's why they contacted me and Vivian Trimble, who was the keyboardist at the time. It was all around that same time, '90, '91, '92. I was playing with the Lunachicks, and I toured with them. I was playing with Luscious Jackson. We were getting our first tour.

After college, I got a job at a photo archive as a photo researcher. My hours were 3:00 p.m. to midnight—conducive to a rock and roll lifestyle. After 5:00 or 6:00 p.m. when my co-workers were gone, I was alone and could use the Xerox machine to make flyers or whatever. It was really the perfect job for someone who's playing music. I worked there for five years and graduated to head researcher. When the second Luscious Jackson tour came along, they were just like, "I think we'll accept your resignation." I was like, "Okay." There was a time in the early days of Luscious Jackson of touring and sleeping on people's floors and all that kind of thing, and not knowing if I made the right decision. But soon, we were able to make a living.

THROWING MUSES HAD MOVED TO BOSTON IN THE MID-1980S TO participate in an "actual scene where people got signed" and embarked on their first, big headlining tour with 4AD label-mates, the Pixies, in 1988. Tanya Donelly met Pixies bassist Kim Deal, and the two started a side project called the Breeders with Josephine Wiggs and drummer Britt Walford. They recorded their debut album, *Pod*, with engineer Steve Albini, and released the album on 4AD. A subsequent "illicit affair" of sorts ensued: Kim planned to leave the Pixies and Tanya left Throwing Muses, but the second Breeders album became Belly's debut album, *Star*.

Tanya Donelly: Meeting Kim Deal and starting to work with her really cemented my identity as a musician. Having my extra-curricular relationship with Kim and the Breeders while I was still in the Muses made me feel like, "Oh, this is something that I can do separate from the framework of Throwing Muses." And it is who I am. The Breeders really made me feel like, "Oh, I'm a musician now." With Kim, it was sort of the freedom that came with doing something with someone else. It made me understand that I was an artist in my own skin, and not just in terms of play-ing with Kristin [Hersh]. Belly's first album, those songs were supposed to be a Breeders album. It was supposed to be the sec-ond Breeders album. And in fact, the demos from Fort Apache for those songs say "Breeders" on them.

Kim came in and did a few of them with me as we were get-ting ready. Kim, at that point, was going to leave the Pixies, and I was going to leave Throwing Muses. It was like an affair. But she stayed with them, and I was anxious to move on. I went back to Newport and recruited musician friends there. Tom and Chris Gorman and Fred Abong, from Throwing Muses, came with me for that first one, and Gail [Greenwood] later. I did have that same sort of posse feeling to that band.

Josephine Wiggs: Before the Perfect Disaster and after Attack of the Puppet People, I was in a band called the Avocados. It was a three-piece most of the time. Later on, we did have another gui-tarist. But to begin with, it was a three-piece, and it was my friend Heidi, who I had met through Floyd. She had never played in a band before and didn't really play an instrument. But her cousin Neal Roxon, he played guitar. He wrote the songs and played gui-tar and sang, and he persuaded her to get a snare drum, and she had, like, a tambourine on a stick. The tambourine was taped to a stand, so she used that like a high hat and then just had a snare drum and maybe a floor tom. She was standing up anyway, you know, kind of primitive, Moe Tucker–style. And because Neal couldn't really play lead guitar, I played a lot of melodic stuff on the bass. So I was, like, filling in, playing melodies on the bass. It was fun. We played locally a bit. And then Neal was friends with the Perfect Disaster, and so we supported them a few times, and there was one occasion where the Perfect Disaster's van had broken down or something and so they called me. My dad had a transit van.

I drove them and all their gear to a couple of shows when their van was broken. And there was one time where I was having to maneuver the van and Phil [Parfitt], the singer, said, "You're really good at reversing." And I have to say, that's the only potentially possibly sexist comment I've ever had in the music world. Never had any experience with sexism at all except for that one little moment where he was thinking that maybe I wouldn't be able to reverse because I was a girl.

So then they were about to go in and make their second album, and they had parted ways with their bass player. They said, "We're making our second album in two weeks. Can you come and play the bass?" So I learned the songs, went in, and recorded in the studio in London. That was, like, the first proper album that I ever made—1987, I think it was. We supported the Pixies, and we had done a fair amount of gigging. We toured with the Jesus and Mary Chain, and at the end of '89, we did shows with the Pixies. So that's how, that's how I met Kim [Deal]. A couple of months later, she had somebody from 4AD call me to ask if I would be interested in playing with her. She and Tanya [Donelly] had a bunch of songs and they both had time off, and they wanted to make a record.

Tanya, Kim, and Britt Walford came to the UK mainly because Tanya was in London with her boyfriend at the time having a holiday with him. Kim and Britt came to my parents' house because I was just living in a shared house, a student house in Brighton. So they came to my parents' house, and we set up in one of the rooms with the drum kits and amps and everything, and that's where we rehearsed *Pod*. I recorded a third album with the Perfect Disaster, and then I decided to leave the Perfect Disaster in hopes that the Breeders might do something.

Donita Sparks: Jennifer Finch saw us play a show, and she muscled her way into the band; she really wanted to be in it, but she didn't even play. She says she played bass, but she didn't. Suzi and I taught her, she was great, she had a lot of moxie and drive, and she knew people. She grew up in LA, so when she joined the band, it started to pick up momentum. She knew one of the founders of Epitaph Records, which was a new label at the time, and they offered to put out our debut album. And then when we got our drummer, Dee [Plakas], in the band, after our first record, that was when things really started to roll, because she's such a great drummer. We were picking up steam anyway, but the addition of Dee was like magic.

Louise Post: Mazzy Star, *She Hangs Brightly*, had just come out. I was a big Cocteau Twins fan and My Bloody Valentine, *Loveless*. And then Belly, *Star*, which is one of my favorite records. Juliana Hatfield was happening, and we both really liked her, and the Boston scene was figuring heavily into our lives, and then *Pod* happened, and we saw the Breeders at the Metro in Chicago and that was life-changing. And then I saw L7 play, and I had never heard of them. I thought the girls in L7 were the roadies setting up the band's gear. And I thought, *God, these guys have really cool girl roadies. They've got a lot of them.* And they strapped on their guitars and started playing and blew my head off, and that was that. Nina and I were compelled to start a female band because of having seen these other groups and because we thought that was the strongest, most feminist thing to do at the time also. But it didn't work out that way.

Shirley Manson: I got a phone call from my A&R guy at Radioactive, Phil Schuster, and he said to me, "Okay, something outrageous has happened. We've just heard from Butch Vig. He's very interested in meeting you about this project he's working on." And I'm like, "Okay. Who's Butch Vig?" And he was like, "Well, he just produced *Nevermind*, he produced *Dirty* by Sonic Youth, he produced Smashing Pumpkins," And I was like, "Oh my God." And of course, I knew all those records, but I'd never paid attention to who produced what.

I took the meeting, but I never thought it would come to anything. I met them in the Landmark Hotel in London, and we all got along very nicely. We had very similar senses of humor. We liked the same kind of music and artists and so on and so forth. They said, "Well, we haven't decided what we're going to do yet. We're thinking of having a multitude of singers. It's been great meeting you. See [you] around." And I was like, "Yeah, great. It was great meeting you. Good luck with your project." I remember saying that very earnestly: "Good luck with your project, no matter how it goes!" I remember leaving them at the corner and going off to my friend's house, switching on the TV, and it was the day that, bless his heart, Kurt Cobain died. It was such a bizarre moment for me, because I felt attached to this experience, having been with Butch an hour before, and he was so involved in the Nirvana story. And I remember feeling like electricity pulsing through me and being so sad about it because Kurt was such a great artist and Nirvana was such an amazing band, but also this bizarre experience of having just met Butch.

A couple of weeks later, I went on tour with Angelfish, who left me in New York in the middle of that tour—we broke up—when I got a phone call from Garbage asking if I wanted to audition.

I was like, "Yeah. I'll get on the next bus. I'll see you tomorrow morning," and it was this weird slide into a new life. I went up to Madison, had my first audition, and then the rest is quite literally my history.

THROUGHOUT THE 1980S, MAGAZINES, COLLEGE-RADIO AIRPLAY, and word of mouth had increased the prominence and highlighted the diversity of alternative rock's distinct styles (and music scenes) like noise pop, indie rock, grunge, and shoegaze. In September 1988, *Billboard* introduced "alternative" into their charting system to reflect the rise of the format across radio stations in the United States by stations like KROQ-FM in Los Angeles and WDRE-FM in New York. These stations were playing music from more underground, independent, and noncommercial rock artists. Several alternative styles achieved mainstream notice, and a few bands, including R.E.M., Sonic Youth, and Jane's Addiction, were signed to major labels. But most alternative bands remained signed to independent labels and received relatively little attention from mainstream radio, television, or newspapers. With the breakthrough of Nirvana and the popularity of the grunge and Brit-pop movements in the 1990s, alternative rock entered the musical mainstream, and many alternative bands became commercially successful.

The release of Nirvana's single "Smells Like Teen Spirit" in September 1991 marked the beginning of the grunge music phenomenon. MTV incessantly played the video, and *Nevermind* was selling four hundred thousand copies a week by Christmas 1991.[3] Its success surprised everyone—the band, their peers, the industry, everyone. *Nevermind* popularized grunge and established the cultural and commercial viability of alternative rock.[4]

The epochal rock revolution has been recategorized, retro-spectively, as a male-centric cultural phenomenon manifest-ing in Seattle, Washington. This isn't entirely true. Nirvana was from Aberdeen and moved to Olympia; as a matter of fact, Kurt Cobain was more affiliated with riot grrrl than any of the bands in this book. Eddie Vedder was a surfer from San Diego who moved north when Pearl Jam needed a lead singer. Per-haps a more poignant observation: a lot of women played in rock bands before the grunge takeover and therefore were an integral part of its process. Some of these women did, in fact, hail from Seattle. Bands like 7 Year Bitch, Calamity Jane, Dickless, and the Gits. In 1983, the late Tina Bell created the sound and lyrical foundation for the grunge genre as lead singer of Bam Bam. Bell was punk as fuck, Black, and female, and despite innovating the grunge sound, she had the misfortune of being way ahead of the curve and entirely forgotten. Gail Ann Dorsey received pushback because she was Black and played rock music (a common theme among Black female rock musicians) at a time when all Black musicians were encouraged to play "Black music"—even Grace Jones. Rock and alternative categories in the '90s may have been sonically diverse, but the categories themselves are rooted in a racist history and were very, very white.[5]

Women in rock lived all over the United States, contrib-uted to various regional scenes and subcultural communities, and their influences ran the gamut. None of them knew one another—there was not some global girls' club—and most made their way to mainstream success through hard work, sac-rifice, and persistence, a pattern that seems to naturally apply to men. Patty Schemel, Shirley Manson, Kate Schellenbach, and Donita Sparks started out early, in the 1980s, and, in the words of bros, paid their dues. Tracy Bonham, Nina Gordon, and

Louise Post are crucial examples of how influential alternative rock was by the mid-'90s, when they were essentially given permission to start their own bands by way of the exceeding visibility and musical diversity of alt-rock artists like the Breeders, L7, Liz Phair, and Mazzy Star. Subsequently, Veruca Salt combined several-part harmonies with sludgy, distorted riffs, and Tracy Bonham didn't hide the fact that she was a classically trained vocalist and violinist. Artistic freedom was the rule.

Women in rock, like men, benefited from college radio and independent record labels, which provided tour support and new avenues for underground artists to reach wider audiences, and acted as a bridge between subculture and the mainstream. Women also benefited from the inherent inclusivity of grunge, which was explicitly anti-sexist, anti-homophobic, and anti-racist. Before it became a mainstream phenomenon, alt-rock subcultures were largely (not always) egalitarian and upheld by feminist men, which made playing women on college radio or signing them to indie labels acceptable—and cool.

Chapter 2

THE WHOLE INDUSTRY DESCENDED ON US

South by Southwest was a pivotal moment and a seminal
show for us because every industry person was there.
And at that moment, it seemed like the whole industry
descended on us and we ended up being courted by almost
every major label just on the virtues of our seven-inch.

—Louise Post, Veruca Salt

L OS ANGELES–BASED ALL-MALE BAND JANE'S ADDICTION
released their first album, *Nothing's Shocking*, on Warner
Records. Their debut is considered a major turning point in the
commercial viability of alternative bands. In 1990, lead singer
Perry Farrell conceived a touring festival featuring a diverse
lineup of alternative artists. In 1991, Dave Grohl attended the
inaugural Lollapalooza festival in Los Angeles, noting how it

changed the mentalities of major labels. Meanwhile, local communities and independent labels nurtured their own alternative subcultural scenes.

Sub Pop is probably the most recognizable label from the era, but Chicago had Drag City and Minty Fresh; L7 released their debut studio album on the Hollywood, California, label Epitaph Records in 1988; Chris Lombardi created Matador Records in his New York City apartment and later signed Liz Phair; Twin/Tone Records signed hometown heroes Babes in Toyland who released *Spanking Machine* in 1990; Hole released their first singles "Retard Girl" and "Dicknail" on Sympathy for the Record Industry in 1990 and 1991; British label Caroline Records reemerged in the United States in 1986 and released the band's debut LP, *Pretty on the Inside*, in 1991; Jay Faires founded Mammoth Records in Chapel Hill, North Carolina, in 1989 and went on to release albums by Blake Babies and Juliana Hatfield (also a member of Blake Babies); Slim Moon and Tinuviel Sampson started Kill Rock Stars in 1991; and British label 4AD signed indie weirdo gang Throwing Muses, the Pixies, the Breeders, and Kristin Hersh.

But Sub Pop founders Jonathan Poneman and Bruce Pavitt were the ones who most successfully capitalized on their scene, which is kind of an oxymoron: punk capitalists. But they essentially created a brand—grunge—and hired British journalist Everett True to cover the "Seattle sound." They produced Lame Fest UK in England, showcasing Nirvana, Tad, and Mudhoney before sending them off on an eight-day tour of Europe. So grunge was just a fabricated talking point, or buzzword, meant to draw attention to Seattle bands. I think it worked.

Not only were there functioning independent record labels, but college radio was to kids who loved alternative music what TikTok is to kids who want to be social media influencers or unlicensed therapists today: important. These radio stations played unsigned bands, signed bands, and most important, local bands. If a local band received a lot of airplay, they would likely get signed to an independent label. Consequently, female-fronted rock bands became part of a mass exodus from indie to major labels and quickly went from playing clubs and touring in minivans to traveling in tour buses and receiving weekly allowances, massive recording advances, and major-label distribution. The process by which women achieved mainstream visibility was really that simple. But the road to forming a functioning band, putting out that first single, and touring the country varied greatly. Artists like Veruca Salt and Tracy Bonham were influenced by seeing bands like the Breeders and L7. Progenitors of the "alternative" genre—Throwing Muses, L7, Hole, Kim Gordon of Sonic Youth—navigated male-dominated music scenes and helped create a buzz, and they broadened pathways for more women in the mid-1990s.

L7 WERE BUSY RECORDING THEIR THIRD STUDIO ALBUM, *BRICKS Are Heavy*, in 1991 when their friends in Nirvana became overnight sensations. Jennifer Finch had even dated Dave Grohl and joked about having to see his face on the covers of magazines while the band was trying to work. Can you imagine seeing your obnoxious ex-boyfriend on the cover of *Rolling Stone*? Ugh. *Bricks Are Heavy* peaked at #160 on the US Billboard 200 and reached #1 on the Heatseekers Albums chart. Engineered by L7 and Butch Vig (he also produced *Nevermind*), the album is more heavily produced and commercial, but still maintains its integrity. *Entertainment Weekly* described the album as "catchy tunes and mean vocals on top of ugly guitars and a quick-but-thick bottom of cast-iron grunge." *NME* (*New Musical Express*) listed it as the thirty-ninth best album of 1992, and in 2015, *SPIN* magazine placed it at #249 on the "300 Best Albums of the Past 30 Years (1985–2014)" list. Before the hit single "Pretend We're Dead" garnered global attention, founding members Donita Sparks and Suzi Gardner struggled to find band members and to make space for themselves in the LA music scene.

Donita Sparks: We went through many years, just the two of us—Suzi [Gardner] and I. Our drummers were always quitting on us, our bass players were always quitting on us. It was just years of struggle, really.

Jennifer [Finch] really wanted to be in a band. She had just moved back to LA, and she convinced me to let her play bass. We taught her, and then she was great, and she had a lot of moxie and a lot of drive. She knew people because she grew up in LA, so when she joined, the band started to pick up momentum. Within two weeks, we had stickers. And it was like, "Oh my God, we have stickers? Whoa, that's huge!" Dee Plakas joined after our first record, and that was when things really started to roll because she's such a great drummer, and that happened in '88.

We did our first national tour opening for Bad Religion in '88, and that was without Dee. And then Dee joined the band in winter of '88, I think. We got involved with the Sub Pop people, and our record came out. We put out a single, and that hit Europe. And suddenly, we were touring Europe, because the Sub Pop Singles Club was so popular. January of 1990 was our Single of the Month Club. We did an EP for Sub Pop that year, and then we got signed to a major label, Slash Records. It was an indie label out of Los Angeles that had a deal with Warner Bros.

BABES IN TOYLAND'S RAUCOUS DEBUT ALBUM, *SPANKING MACHINE*, landed them a slot on Sonic Youth's European tour. The band are featured in the documentary/tour diary *1991: The Year Punk Broke*. Their second album, *Fontanelle*, was their first major-label release, having returned to the States a respected, powerful force in the underground. The band joined the Lollapalooza tour in 1993 and released an EP, a compilation album, and their last full-length album, *Nemesisters* (1995).

Lori Barbero: We had Twin Towers booking, who worked with Sonic Youth and Madonna and Patti Smith and just all of these big bands. And we had a lawyer, Richard Grabel, who was Sonic Youth's and I think Madonna's lawyer. There were changes like that where we wanted to make sure that we had all our i's dotted and our t's crossed. But honestly, really, we still toured in vans, and maybe we got a manager here and there. But we aren't very good at people telling us what to do. I would imagine, Kat [Bjelland] and I are both Sagittarians, and we have never been very receptive to that kind of criticism or help. When someone is telling us what we're supposed to be doing instead of asking or suggesting, we're like, "Oh, hell no."

Jill Emery: I mean, I can really appreciate the small labels, but at the same time, when I was doing these van tours, I was sleeping on people's floors, couches, whatever. But when you get to a major label, it turns into a tour bus. You get your own bunk. And then it got to the point, not with Hole but with Mazzy Star, I was very lucky to get my own room. It was great. And that was the great part. But yeah, you do want your music to be heard. And yeah, I want to make money because this is my craft, this is my art. But money, it wasn't really flowing. I mean, it wasn't great. I did quit before Hole signed to the major label. And people were like, "Stick it out." I'm like, "No, the money's not worth it." I'm fine, but it wasn't worth it. It was too traumatizing.

But I loved playing. I loved expressing myself. And so, with Hole, it was a great vehicle. It was great. But as you know, it was very difficult. I can remember, this was towards the end, but I think we were in Scotland on tour and something, Courtney was just saying something to me, she was just pushing my buttons. And then we started kind of fighting a bit, and then, she dumped sugar on my head, and I was like, "That's it." I remember we were playing with Daisy Chainsaw, and I was just so pissed. I was hanging out with them, and that was the night the girl shaved my head. I go, "I'm not washing this sugar out. Just fucking shave my head." And she had her head shaved, too, this girl. How come I can't remember her name? Anyway, but Daisy Chainsaw, that was the band. And that was like, "I'm done with this band."

I gave my notice after we got back home, and the lawyers called me and said I'm under contract to play this last show at the Whisky. I played it, but if you see pictures—my friend Lindsay Brice took pictures—and I was in this dress that looked like I just came out of an insane asylum, and I had those sleeper things on my head, and my head was shaved, and I was just like, "Ah," and playing with my back to the band. It was just pure anger. I'm not angry anymore, but I can call up that feeling.

When I got home, I put out an ad in the *Recycler* and I said, "Bassist looking to start a band. Influences: Marianne Faithfull, Mazzy Star, and Black Sabbath." And Mazzy Star calls me, and I'm like, "What?" They're like, "Hey, you want to come down and jam a bit?" I'm like, "Yeah, I'll be there." And of course, he had a great studio. David Roback, he was an archivist with instruments. He just had it.

I remember thinking, *Wow, I can't believe I'm playing these songs that I love.* And I'm not great. I'm a slow learner, but once I get it, I'm on it. So that was really cool. And then I didn't hear back, and I remember Hope [Sandoval] tells the story, "Oh yeah, you said, 'Can I take off my shoes?'" I was like, "I don't remember that." And she's like, "And we all just laughed," because they were very quiet. It was opposite of Hole.

I didn't hear from them maybe for a couple weeks. And then they called me and said, "Hey, we're playing this show with Red House Painters." And it was just a club. And they're like, "You want to play?" I'm like, "I don't think I know the songs that well." And they're like, "Just come and play." I'm like, "Okay, but I'm going to be staring at your hands to see chord changes." And I played the show. And then from there on, I went on tour with them for that record, and they paid me. I was a hired musician, so I didn't get royalties, but I got paid when we toured.

Patty Schemel: I tried out for a few different bands in San Francisco and played some shows. I was in a band called Dumbhead with Debbie Shane—she was Dale Crover's [the Melvins] girlfriend. The Melvins had moved to San Francisco, so I had some friends around. The Melvins were a big influence on Nirvana. Courtney met Kurt and they became a couple, and Courtney was looking for a female drummer for her band, Hole. Kurt mentioned that he knew me, he reached out to Dylan Carlson, Dylan called me, and that's how I ended up auditioning for Hole in '91.

I went to our rehearsal space and practiced everything from *Pretty on the Inside* and the bootleg stuff and then went down to LA. I met Eric [Erlandson], and he told me they practiced at Jabberjaw, an all-ages club on West Pico. I got there, set my drums up on the stage, and we just started playing some of the songs that were on *Pretty on the Inside*. We did the Wipers song "Over the Edge," and Eric said, "That's how that song should be played," which was a compliment. I would find out later Eric does not give compliments. That was my first introduction to him and to the world on a bigger scale as a performer and a musician. It's that cliché of a big fish in a little pond, so really getting rightsized about my playing and what kind of work needed to be done, which, on the flip side, caused more drinking and more insecurity.

Courtney showed up late, and Kurt came, and we sat around and talked about bands and our influences. We wrote songs, made up stuff, and then Courtney said, "If you don't have a place to stay, you can stay at our place." They had an apartment on Spaulding in Hollywood. I went, and there were records laid out everywhere—they just listened to records nonstop and made fanzines. I remember they put on Mazzy Star, *She Hangs Brightly*. Courtney and I talked about women that we were influenced by in bands. Frightwig was a huge band for me, and she knew the girls in Frightwig. We talked about living in San Francisco and hearing these bands, and Babes in Toyland, Pink Cat, and how important the Runaways were. It felt good to talk about music and find that we had the same interests and the same style.

So that's how playing in Hole began. I turned twenty-five the day of the audition. I planned to come back the following weekend, but it was the Rodney King verdict, the riots were happening, and everybody was on lockdown. I finally made it back down to work on stuff, and then I started living with Kurt and Courtney in LA. The first song I recorded with the band was "Beautiful

Son." That was an EP we recorded in Seattle with Jack Endino, who I'd worked with before.

Hole was already signed to a major label, and at that point, the band had money to live. The first thing I did was quit my job at a medical supply warehouse, and then I lived off my little record-label salary and dedicated every day to learning all their songs and writing songs for *Live Through This.*

THE GIRLY-SOUND RECORDINGS GAVE LIZ PHAIR THE OPPORTUnity to record *Exile in Guyville*, but her demos possess an unparalleled charm in the unbelievably shitty recording quality, intelligent lyrics, vocal range, and unique guitar playing. Some of my favorites never made it onto *Exile*—namely, "Ant in Alaska" and "Love Song," a six-minute confessional that starts out with Liz Phair snark: "This is another story about love / What a surprise." You can hear her "developing as both a lyricist and musician." It's strikingly similar in character to *Guyville*'s "Shatter," one of the most devastating songs Phair ever wrote.[1]

Liz Phair: I went to the Art Institute of Chicago, finished my degree at Oberlin, came back, was interning for Ed Paschke, and living at home. And I decided I was going to make a go of it with this music thing, because due to paid effort, I was receiving envelope after envelope—this is a very shameful part of my life, I feel really bad about it. I confess it, so I'm not running away— but because I was in my research phase, I would receive unsolicited money from people who were like, "'Can I get a Girly-Sound cassette?' And I'm like, 'Who are you?'" I'd take the money and go down to the bars. It was research. I wouldn't have had *Guyville* without this research. They were patrons of mine before crowdfunding. It allowed me to get a move in the music circle, the downtown music scene, and if people really want these cassettes, I should make an actual album. And that's how it began, really. So, it was fan-driven, fan campaign.

I was also goaded into making the tape in the first place while I was living in San Francisco by a very talented singer-songwriter whose name, for some reason, completely blanking. I'll figure it out. I got by with a little help from my friends, because I was around so many creative people from Oberlin, and it didn't take much professionalism to enter indie rock. The whole point of alternative music had grown from the punk ethos that if you had something to say and a shitty instrument, you can get up on stage and just pour your hearts out, just go for it. There was this sort of thrasher mentality of "I dare you." To say that I would've worked in music without the "I dare you" factor is just wrong. The "I dare you" was so present at that time in my life in so many ways. In the romantic sense, it makes me sad, because I think of men being like, "I dare you." But "I dare you," even in the workplace, even to be a woman in a male workplace was an "I dare you." Even my parents saying, "Oh, you're going to leave our fold that we have invested in you. We gave you an opportunity to be in society." Like, "You could be the American dream, and we invested in you to be that. And you're going to go out and just throw that back in our face? I dare you." Every part of my life is "I dare you."

I didn't realize at the time that bedroom pop was having its beginning at the exact same time because of the technology. But I was right there on that vanguard of home-bedroom pop singer. Everyone can yawn and roll their eyes, but there was an element of being in the right place at the right time. I think the female voice in the indie rock and the punk rock scene was having a moment, was having a visibility moment. But I also think that because I was trained as a visual artist and because I was fresh out of college, fresh out of that competitive realm where—in senior year of college, I was competing with professionals in my line. I was at that exact age where you have the most good stuff poured into you with your education and the least stuff taken out of you by the marketplace. And the fact that I was visible to Matador at all because of my friend in New York, who'd been a friend of one of my roommates, Greta. He encouraged me to write songs. And when I sent him a tape of my Girly-Sound stuff that I recorded in San Francisco, he made tape after tape after tape and sent them to people. Girly-Sound was a goof, a fun, goofy thing to do, and an outlet. I was very lucky to have met him; lucky that he made copies of my cassette for all these people and cool magazines and zines. He was doing my marketing without my knowledge. I approached Matador to sign with them using these songs, these Girly-Sound cassettes that I had recorded in my private life, that I had no professional aspiration for; it was just some stuff I did. I was going to be a visual artist. This entire time until I became famous, I had had one dream since childhood—to be a visual artist. And I was interning for Ed Paschke, a very avant-garde painter in Chicago. I was interning for Leon [Golub] and Nancy [Spiro]. I was dead serious about being a visual artist.

VERUCA SALT WERE PART OF THE SECOND WAVE OF THE ALTERNA-tive music phenomenon and had the fortune of seeing women playing loud, distorted rock music, live and in person. Cofounders Nina Gordon and Louise Post grew up singing show tunes and folk songs. They idolized Prince and Wendy and Lisa. By the mid-1980s, Sonic Youth was on everyone's radar, and Kim Gordon was exalted as the "godmother of noise." Kim Deal was a visible, ethereal presence in the Pixies and began performing with her own side project, the Breeders, in 1990. L7 had released two albums by that time and were an active, touring, all-female band that made an enormous impression on the fledgling Chicago duo as they transitioned from acoustic folk to alternative rock.

Louise Post: When I graduated college, I went and visited a friend in Israel for six weeks. I had just been to Chicago, visiting. I went up for a weekend earlier that summer right after graduating and I went home to St. Louis, drove to Chicago with a friend, and I saw another childhood friend of mine in a theater company called the New Criminals. They were doing this really punk rock improvisational theater—basically a bastardization of Théâtre du Soleil.

I really wanted to be a part of it, and I logged that and went to Israel, and when I came back, I moved to Chicago. I just threw all my bags in the back seat of my car and drove up. I remember being on this solo journey listening to Pink Floyd for some reason. I rented a room from my big sister's friend in the Wrigleyville/Lakeview area and got a job waiting tables. I joined this theater company and I also continued seeing bands and writing songs, and this was a critical juncture for me: this theater company—that was so revelatory and so life-changing for me, such an incredible experience—was run by guys, and they had just done a series of plays that had very few female parts in it. For the last play, there were only two female roles—really only one. I was an understudy or double cast for the main role, and I was also in the band for the play, and at the end of that, I realized I really needed to run my own show, whatever that was. I had also done headshots and gone and met an agent and showed him the headshots, and he said, "Well, you know, we would probably use this photo of you because you can't see your crooked tooth," and I was like, "I have a crooked tooth? What?" That epitomized why I didn't want to go into acting. I didn't want people pointing out my supposed flaws of which I was unaware, like blissfully unaware, and it was around that time that the guy I was seeing said, "I really see you as a singer-songwriter," and he suggested I write a song every day. I set about writing a song every day, and I went into a studio where my brother was recording in St. Louis, and he recorded a few songs for me, and that New Year's Eve, my boyfriend and I had a little gathering. Lili Taylor was there. She was a Chicago actor gone big, and she was back in town.

At one point, I put the songs on—the cassette that I had of the stuff I had just recorded—and she came directly over to me and said, "Is this you?" I said, "Yeah." And she said, "You have to meet my friend Nina. She just got back from school. She's an incredible singer, and she writes songs, too."

Nina Gordon: I moved back to Chicago after Tufts. I worked in an art gallery that represented a lot of really inspiring female artists. I was twenty-one, working at the gallery and, like, seeing my life in terms of art and thinking about going to graduate school in art history but secretly wishing, and watching MTV, and looking at magazines and feeling like, "Ugh, that's what I really want to do." I did have a great passion for art, too, and a lot of the artists we represented at the gallery were women who inspired me to make art, write songs, or just to be sort of brave and courageous in terms of what I was willing to expose of myself.

I had an acoustic guitar in my little apartment in Chicago and an electric guitar but no amp and no distortion pedal. I would go and see every band that came through town—this was a common experience that Louise and I had—I went to see Wendy and Lisa perform. They played in Prince's band originally but made records on their own with other women. So I saw this stage filled with women playing their instruments and singing and was totally, completely blown away and inspired. It still felt out of reach to me, but it felt a little bit closer. I had a little four track that I would record songs on. I didn't really know what I was doing, but it was enough. At least enough to be able to hear what my songs sounded like, and I could sing harmony with myself. But all I wanted to do was sing harmony with someone else.

I put some ads in the local paper, the *Chicago Reader*, looking for people to play with. I met with a few dudes who came to my apartment—totally not cool at all, like ridiculous experiences. No one I connected with, I was just like, "No way." I knew I couldn't do it alone. I didn't have the ability to self-promote. I wasn't the kind of person who was going to go out and busk and make it. It was passion, but there was so much fear around that passion. And then the Lili thing happened. She came to town; she and I were talking. We had a lot of similar tastes in music. We shared all our music with each other, made mixtapes for each other all the time, and she said, "You really gotta do this. You're so good at this. Why aren't you doing this?" And I said, "I just can't. I can't do it on my own. I don't have it in me." She came over on New Year's Eve after she'd been at Louise's house, and she said, "I met this woman who is writing songs, you guys need to meet, and promise me you'll call her." It was because Louise forced me to go out in public in front of people and go into the studio—and she's still forcing me to do it now.

Louise Post: We recorded everything. I was a crazy fanatical logger, so I had a notebook in which I logged everything we did, and that's what got me through as I was waiting tables—I worked at this jazz club called Andy's in downtown Chicago on State [Street] and Hubbard—and in between bringing out food to people, I would just log what we had done at practice and what we were doing the next day.

Nina Gordon: Louise forced me to play open mics. I have a videotape of the two of us when we first started getting together, three days a week, when Louise was logging. We're singing folk songs, we've both got acoustic guitars, we could have totally been, you know, a different version of the Indigo Girls or something. We were always heavy in terms of the content, but we were playing strummy guitar. And then we went to see the Breeders after *Pod* came out.

Louise Post: When I was in college, a friend turned me onto the Pixies' *Doolittle*, Brian Eno's *Another Green World*, and then Jane's Addiction's *Nothing's Shocking* happened. I saw that tour in Chicago, and that changed my life. Nina and I grew up on Prince and had always been singing the mad harmonies in Prince. Jim [Shapiro] is also a big fan, and those harmonies play into what we do a lot. And then Belly's first album, *Star*, came out. Juliana Hatfield was happening, and we both really liked her, and the Boston scene was figuring heavily into our lives. Then we saw the Breeders at the Metro in Chicago, and that was life-changing, and that was band-changing.

Nina Gordon: I mean, seeing the Breeders—there was a moment where it was just like, "You know what, we can do this all day long and it's beautiful," but there was this feeling of, like, we want to stand up, we don't want to sit on stools. We want to stand up, we want to stomp on our pedals, you know? We want to do this! We can do this. And I also wondered, can our voices be heard over the din of loud electric guitars? And yes, the Breeders were doing it, My Bloody Valentine was doing it. I had written "Cock of Nothing." That was the first song I wrote on electric with distortion.

Louise Post: We were compelled to start a female band because of having seen these other groups and because we thought that was the strongest, most feminist thing to do at the time also. And coming out of being in a theater company that was predominantly male, though there were tons of really talented women in the theater company, I really wanted it to be, you know, force by numbers.

Nina Gordon: But Steve [Lack] responded to an ad we put in the paper. He called and said, "I really like your influences. I'm not a girl." He came to Louise's apartment in Chicago, where we were practicing, and he was great. He's such a good bass player. But that was later. Our first show was at a club called Phyllis' Musical Inn. Louise booked it because she did everything. Louise was the one that got us to record a four-song demo with some weird dude down on the South Side.

Louise Post: Brad Wood, our producer, was there at that show. He came to see this band called Elliot with whom we shared a practice space, and we were opening for them.

Nina Gordon: This dude named Jim Powers came to our third show, and he had a little indie label called Minty Fresh. After that show, he wanted to sign us. He wanted to do a single with us, a seven-inch [vinyl record], and so we said, "Great! Let's do it." And we got a lawyer to broker that deal, and we didn't have a manager. And then we decided, I guess, that we wanted to do it with Brad? Maybe Jim Powers knew Brad? I think that's what it was.

Louise Post: He had a deal with Brad. Brad was recording a seven-inch for his label, and so we went in to record with Brad and brought "Seether" and "All Hail Me," and we were just going to do the seven-inch with him. We had just demoed "Seether" at another studio, and we were like, "All right, let's do this song." But very quickly, that turned into a full-length album, and we were going to do it in like two weeks, but we were not that kind of band. So we ended up going in over the course of the next few months while in between touring. We were touring in a van around the Midwest and the East Coast, and we did South by Southwest. South by Southwest was a pivotal moment and a seminal show for us because every industry person was there. And at that moment, it seemed like the whole industry descended on us and we ended up being courted by almost every major label just on the virtues of our seven-inch. "Seether" came out that summer, someone at *Hits* magazine sent it to someone at KROQ, Jim Powers was working the England angle and so while we were finishing our record up, "Seether" hit and became a big single in England and then in Los Angeles and all over the States. We were trying to hold the song back because the record wasn't ready yet. It wasn't coming out until September, but as it happened, it was all good, of course, and it became what it became, and it got us on a tour bus, and the record came out in September, and we went on tour with Hole in '94.

As a young teenager, I assumed that being played on the radio meant that you were getting paid. I never imagined the women in Luscious Jackson or Throwing Muses having side jobs. For all I know, Tanya Donelly was my waitress during one of our family trips to Boston. Starting a band, recording, and touring didn't pay the bills unless you had the fortune/misfortune of touring constantly. I grew up in Massachusetts and Rhode Island, where college radio was an important network for local bands until the early 2000s. Having conquered college radio, been signed to an independent label, and touring consistently, bands like Throwing Muses and Belly had an opportunity to sign with Warner Bros. Obviously, this meant a steadier income. Major labels began to decimate independent labels by offering astronomical advances. The catch was, of course, that bands had to pay all extraneous costs back to the label to break even on a record.

Tanya Donelly: In Throwing Muses, I worked as a waitress in the off time, or I worked at Newbury Comics for years. And then just started kind of touring a lot. And once we signed with Warner Bros., things did get easier. We were still working, but we had tour support. So then when we were on the road, we were supported. And we did a lot of touring as a result.

We really, really relied on the college radio network. And there was such a thing back then. That was the web back then. And if you didn't have that, those little dots lining up and those lights going off, then it was playing, getting a good opening slot, getting college radio.

With Belly, once Belly happened, that re-signing was significant because it was on the heels of our first record, *Star*. We signed it after the record had already taken off. It was when my contract came up, and then I re-signed to that point. So that was a fortuitous moment. But again, if you wanted to really be making a living, you had to tour all the time. There was an eighteen-month tour at one point when I was in Belly, just to make sure that we were in the black at the end of it. So I wasn't working at that point other than the music, and that kind of extended a little into my solo life.

MELISSA AUF DER MAUR DOESN'T KNOW THIS, BUT SHE STOLE MY job. In 1994, I recorded myself playing shitty bass lines into a tape recorder and sent it to Hole's management—or maybe it was a fan club. Courtney Love had initiated a worldwide search for a new bassist after the untimely death of Kristen Pfaff in 1994. I didn't get the job, and I was only thirteen, but whatever. While I was fumbling around the fret board, Auf der Maur had already made a name for herself as bassist of the band Tinker. She had also caught the attention of Smashing Pumpkins' Billy Corgan. She pulled a similar stunt in 1992, mailing a letter to Corgan, although her inquiry ended with Tinker opening for the Pumpkins, and mine ended with me resenting the supercool red-head who ended up stealing the fame and fortune (ha!) I felt I was entitled to.

Melissa Auf der Maur: I found these guys who were around my age, and we started my first band, Tinker. The joke is that our eighth show ever was opening for Smashing Pumpkins during the *Siamese Dream* tour because I wrote a letter to the PO box saying, "Hi, Billy, remember me? I met you in 1991, when my roommate threw a beer bottle at you. I finally started a band. Can I open for you?" And miraculously, he got the letter, and Tinker opened for him. We opened for Swervedriver, which was another one of my favorite bands, in front of three thousand people. I had only played, like, tiny clubs with like forty people before that. And I walked offstage, and Billy Corgan said, "Melissa, you're better than my bass player. You're gonna be in my band one day." And first I thought, (A) *D'arcy [Wretzky] is pretty good, and* (B) *wow. Even if I never see you again, I just got the biggest vote of confidence from one of my heroes.*

Three months later, Billy told Courtney about me. Kristen Pfaff had died. And they were on an international search for a bass-player replacement. Courtney and the whole band were living in this horrendous wake of loss from Kurt and then Kristen. Billy Corgan called, said, "Hey, I got good news and great news. I'm playing Lollapalooza. We're gonna be in Montreal next month. You should come. I have a day off; we can have lunch. The great news is, you're gonna join my friend Courtney Love's band, Hole." And I said, "No, I'm not. [*laughs*] No, I have my own band here, and I'm preparing to apply for my master's next year."

So he came to town. We had lunch. We walked through this park in front of my mother's house. And he said, "Why don't you want to play in the biggest female rock band ever and pretty much never have to work?" And I said, "That doesn't sound fun to me. No thank you." A week or so later, my roommate said, "Courtney Love called for you." I said, "Really? Did she leave a number?" I didn't call her back. Then, the next day, she left a message on my machine. She called a few times before we spoke—it was late night, and I remember clearly my bedroom décor, lots of gold and velvet.

She said, "Hi. Why don't you want to join my band?" I said, "I have a lot going on, actually. I'm in school, and I have a band." And she said, "Can you just get on the plane to Seattle this weekend and tell me to my face? Just come meet us." And she was super convincing, and it was a good point, like perhaps I should not just say no, although I obviously had a pretty strong gut reaction, which was that it seemed like a very heavy situation. But also, I didn't want to be a famous musician. I also didn't want to necessarily be making a statement for women in rock music.

But I flew across the country. I listened to *Live Through This* on cassette. The album was just coming out. I was a DJ, so I always got advance copies for my promoter friends. I listened to it all the way to Seattle, and I thought, *Oh, these are pretty easy songs.* When I landed, I came down the escalator, looked at these women; they were all smiling. Before I said hello, I saw them, and in my gut, I knew I had to do this. I saw these women and just saw the hole that they were literally trying to fill. And I couldn't say no. And I realized I had to do it. My first show with Hole was August 1994, at the Reading Festival in front of sixty-five thousand people. That was the ninth concert of my life.

Tracy Bonham: I had a boyfriend who was an incredible drummer, and we were in a wedding band together. I was late for registration one day at Berklee, and I signed up for this thing, GB Ensemble. It ended up meaning *General Business*, which was another way of saying *wedding band*. This is when I knew Berklee was not right for me. I was like, "I'm taking a class in how to sing, 'The bride cuts the cake, the bride cuts the cake.'" But I was like, "I'm getting credit for this, but I'm also paying for this. So I'm out."

My boyfriend was really instrumental in getting me to write, because he was in like seven different bands, and they were all doing well in Boston, and they were all really different and unique. He told me, "You can do this. You're not going to be a wedding singer for the rest of your life. Please, you're too good for this."

One day, he went off to a gig, and he just kind of gave me this little exercise. He was like, "Why don't you take that guitar, take the three chords that you already know, and write a song? And then when I come back, why don't you play it for me?" I took the challenge, and I wrote this song, and that was kind of the start of it. I have him to thank. I never really give him enough credit. So I had written "Mother Mother," but I didn't have a chorus. And he and I went to a practice room one day, and he was just like, "Just keep going with it." And all of a sudden, we're just jamming, and then we're like, "Bump, bump." And I'm screaming, "Everything is fine!" It came from the sky, and I started laughing. I thought, *Oh my God, I could never do that. That's weird. I'm screaming.* And he thought it was great.

I was a musician all my life, and at that time, I was honing my craft and trying to figure out who I was and what I wanted to do. When I did start to kind of create a buzz with my three-song demo tape, it happened very fast because the timing was right. Everyone was looking to Boston because there was a lot of stuff happening at the time. And female rock artists were kind of the hot ticket, too. So I was in the right place at the right time. At the time, I wouldn't have wanted to admit that. I thought it was all based on my merit, but I think there was a lot of luck involved.

I only had three songs, started playing gigs, and then made that demo tape. The demo tape landed in the hands of somebody, and then it went to New York, and then I had to write more songs because some high-powered people were coming to see me. I told them, "I don't have a record worth of material." And they were like, "Well, you better get on it." And then, "Here, we're going to meet this lawyer," and "You want to meet this publisher." It was a real crash course. I dropped out of Berklee in '91. Now I did the wedding band for a couple of years, but in '93, I started putting that demo tape together, then by '95, I had an EP out, which was subsidized by my major label that gave me a lot of money to make some albums. So yeah, it really was fast.

Josephine Wiggs: It was fun touring with Nirvana and playing those big stadium shows with them in '93. And it was fun doing Lollapalooza, even though at the time it was like, "Oh my fucking God." Just, you know, it felt like we were being ground under the heel of something or other. It was really arduous in some ways, but in other ways, it was something that's never going to happen again. There was a time when my mother and my sister came to visit me in New York, and I took them to the top of the Empire State Building and was showing them around or whatever, and somebody was like, "Hey, aren't you Josephine from the Breeders?" You know, in front of my mom and my sister and, of course, it was supercool. And then, there'd be times where Kate [Schellenbach] and I would be sitting in a restaurant in New York, and someone would tap you on the shoulder, and say, "Hey, aren't you . . . ?"

THE GRUNGE IDEOLOGY WAS ANATHEMA TO THE DANDY WARHOLS. By the mid-1990s, Zia McCabe had no interest in the plaid, dirty, self-loathing ethos of what was, by then, a mainstream cultural phenomenon. McCabe, singer-guitarist Courtney Taylor-Taylor, and lead guitarist Peter Holmström endorsed a more Dionysian approach to creativity: drinking, partying, nudity. The result was three-minute pop songs that brilliantly critiqued the shortcomings of grunge and its mainstream commodification.

Zia McCabe (the Dandy Warhols): I was eighteen in 1993. I had dropped out of college, met Courtney [Taylor-Taylor] and Peter [Holmström]. Peter's parents lived up in the West Hills [Portland, Oregon], and they had a solar-heated pool and a wine cellar. We went on this wonderful, exciting, I think six weeks of playing music all the time, playing shows, going back to Pete's parents', having huge parties, everyone naked in the pool. I mean, I just couldn't believe what was going on and having the time of my life. And then the shows just kept coming. And then now we're going to go to San Francisco. I'm like, "We're going to play outside of our city? We've made it."

Each increment felt like, "Oh, this is all I need," you know? "We sold out little Luna?" Well, my life was complete. We went on a US tour in a van, opening for Love and Rockets. It was this wonderful feeling of everything that happened was not in such rapid succession that you couldn't enjoy it, but spread out just perfectly to where if life ended right there, I would have felt I'd made it further than I ever imagined, and we were always one step beyond what I could imagine. And that's an exciting way to live. 'Cause it's like, this is Christmas every day. Pretty soon, we were flying somewhere. My twentieth birthday was our first trip and my first time in an airplane. My first time in a hotel where they turn down your bed. I thought they were talking about a thermostat. Like these are the things that were happening to me. The world was opening up at the same time the band was finding success. So the sense of wonder was just like nonstop. My twenty-first birthday was our first trip to London.

The music scene in the mid-'90s was grunge bands. It was a lot of angst. It was a lot of people being mad at their parents, mad at whoever, and yelling over three chords. Not a lot of attention being paid to beauty and sensuality. We came on the scene in Portland as these hedonists that missed lounge culture. I was too young to miss lounge culture, but in theory, I wanted velvet and candles, not cement and knees scabs. We were this relief to what was going on, which is what the Dandy Warhols have always done.

But there were some other cool things going on in the smaller scenes. And of course, there was the riot grrrl movement. I never super fit in to that scene, especially once I started playing in the Dandy Warhols. I loved the scene, but I felt excluded. I would bring my boyfriend, which caused points against you. But I felt like I was probably dating feminists. I mean, they wanted to go to the shows. It seemed like it'd be fine. I think that my way of dealing with the way a woman fits into things was just being more of a dude. And looking back on it now, quite sexist in my own way. And that's a way that a lot of women get through being in a man's world is just being kind of misogynistic themselves. In my naive way of coping, I wasn't embracing the movement that they were pushing. And so it makes sense that I wasn't totally included. I didn't really get it.

Being on the independent label was like a four-page contract. It was just very fun and free and easy. And like I said, I felt like, "We made it; we're on a label." We put out our album exactly the way we wanted to and recorded to tape. And Thor Lindsay from Tim/Kerr Records got this bidding war going. And it was during the dying days of the major-label scene. He got them so riled up that they had to have us. We milked that period and the trips to New York and the tickets to music-awards shows

and all these crazy expensive dinners. We took full advantage
of it. We finally settled on Capitol Records. Perry Watts-Russell
is just such a cool dude. And he's who talked us into signing,
and the Capitol building is so cool looking.

BEFORE I BECAME AWARE OF COLLEGE RADIO, MAINSTREAM ROCK
radio and MTV's 120 *Minutes* were my pathways to alternative
music. In New England, WBCN and WFNX (Boston, Massachusetts) and WBRU (Providence, Rhode Island) played bands that
had "made it," like Hole, the Breeders, and Luscious Jackson. If I
wanted to hear something on the radio, I would call the request
line. I might be solely responsible for getting Veruca Salt on the
radio before "Volcano Girls" was released in '97. I also remember
requesting a song by some band called Toad the Wet Sprocket,
but I don't remember why. But all these bands started out on
college radio. Before the commercialization of the internet—
and I can't even imagine this now—a "buzz" was akin to going
viral on social media. People dubbed cassette tapes, gave them
to friends; enter college radio airplay, followed by an indie label
scooping an artist up, and if the band showed any commercial
promise, the major labels swooped in. And while everyone was
trying their best to be famous, to create careers that were sup-
portable, it was absolutely not cool to pursue fame and fortune.
Kurt Cobain popularized the notion that being successful meant
selling out—even after his band did just that. This was another
unfortunate idea I absorbed and took very seriously as I pursued
my own career as an ethically unfamous, yet economically stable
musician.

Chapter 3

THE HARD THING WAS ALWAYS THE PRESS

> The hard thing was always press and how, from our perspective, a fun photo shoot turned into some kind of litmus test as to what we were saying . . . These moments that felt light took on this weight that was insupportable.
>
> —Tanya Donelly

IN 1991, JOURNALIST BARNEY HOSKYNS WROTE THAT ANGRY girls with electric guitars had "highjacked rock and roll" and that these "psycho babes from hell" were symptomatic of a new wave of post-feminist expression.[1] This article appeared in *Vogue*, just to give you a sense of how widespread and mainstream the alternative genre had become. In his 1979 book, *Subculture: The Meaning of Style*, Dick Hebdige provides an account of how the mainstream media deal with youth subcultures.

According to this narrative, youth cultures emerge seemingly spontaneously "from the streets," from outside the capitalist economy. They are then inevitably co-opted by the mainstream, diluted, and commodified. Radical bands are seen to lose their edge as they are signed to major record labels; entrepreneurs soften street fashions as they package them for mainstream high-street consumers; leaders of the style are nominated and often endowed with additional glamour and charisma. Media plays a key role here, albeit veering erratically from fascination with taboo behavior to melodramatic "moral panic." In the '90s, the media played an important role in positioning women as arbiters of a new feminism, while also laying the ground-work for the eventual backlash. The '90s witnessed an explosion of different forms of femininity, a conflation of styles, sounds, genres, and aesthetics that left the media scratching its head. Radio, MTV, and music magazines shaped public opinion but had a difficult time corralling and categorizing these rock women—and the media loves putting women in categorical boxes.

L7 were hard rock, were androgynous, and deliberately chose a gender-neutral band name; Shirley Manson was a little bit goth, a little bit pop, and 100 percent opinionated; Liz Phair wasn't loud, but she was sexual and explicit; Courtney Love and Kat Bjelland screamed and thrashed their guitars in tattered vintage, lipstick-smeared fury; Kristin Hersh was the nice mom, cerebral, genius, and progenitor of modern indie rock; Alanis Morissette emerged in 1995 with hair in her face and a unique vocal affect unveiled in her single "You Oughta Know," exemplifying rage and vulnerability. For a glorious moment, she made being pissed off—and going down on your significant other in a movie theater—cool, although still unhygienic.

Mass media, whether it's aware of it or not, internalizes institutional values while operating under the illusion that it is free, objective, and unbiased. It employs strategies, rooted in the coloniality of gender, women, and women's work and perpetuates myths that we consider natural or innate—myths like (1) rock is masculine, rebellious, and antiestablishment; (2) women are predisposed to compete; (3) women in rock are a novelty or phenomenon; (4) mass media subscribes to gendered categorizations; and (5) mass media preserves the male gaze.[2]

Using this logic, for example, an unwed, childless, hard-rocking woman becomes a spectacle, while child-rearing rock women become dangerous aberrations to our collective understandings of what a wife and mother should be. Women, by virtue of their biology, do not fit into the rock mold, which is all about cock, sex, and masculine sexual prowess. Some, like Courtney Love and Kristin Hersh, were young wives and mothers who upended that revisionist ideology. Hersh went on to have four children and lost custody of her eldest due in part to how she was portrayed in the media (mentally ill) and for being unsuitably employed.

Kristin Hersh: I've been made to look bad for just being a mother in a band so much so that they took my son away. It was easy to make me look bad: a history of mental illness, a rock band, traveling. I'm actually a really good mother. We have a nuclear family, yet they will not forgive me for that one lousy thing, which is that I can't give up my band. The good rock journalists would note the onstage/offstage schism. Basically, their thrust was, "Look at this sweet girl or nice mom lady, and then watch what happens onstage." And that's true, and it's a better story. The Warner Bros. take on what I was, was that I was too ugly and too smart, so that means you are difficult to work with because you're not malleable and you're not marketable. They want someone dumb and hot, and that's not that different from a lot of popular culture, so I probably should have expected it, but music was my religion, and I couldn't imagine that someone would crap all over it like that.

IN 1991, A JOURNALIST FOR *NME* PUBLISHED A BRIEF ARTICLE ABOUT Throwing Muses, written from the perspective of a therapist speaking (him) to a client (Hersh) using every cliché regarding mental illness, from hearing voices to channeling demonic energy.[3]

Kristin Hersh: I was like the poster child for bipolar disorder for twenty years. I didn't mean to tell anyone, but my record label took me out of the hospital to fly me to London and do a press tour, which no one thought I could do, so they put me in Ivo's [Watts-Russell] house, who ran our label, 4AD.

I lived in his house, and journalists would come there and interview me. I wasn't allowed to say anything about where I had just been—on suicide watch—not that I would have wanted to, but it was hard. I was not in a great place, and I had just lost custody of my son, and I was having to answer questions about music, which are often too intense or too shallow. And intense I couldn't handle, and shallow would just be so off base it would make me angry, but like I said, I'm very, very nice, so for two weeks, I was very, very nice, and then these two writers called the Stud Brothers, who are actually brothers and amazing music writers, and good friends, they were the last interview. I had been keeping it together until they got there, and they sat down, and their first question was, "Are you okay?" because they saw something wasn't right. Photographers had been up in my face doing all these photo shoots, and nobody had brought it up or had seen it, and when they said that, I broke down. I told them as friends what had happened, and they said, "We're your friends, and that's how you were speaking to us, the tape recorder was on, but we respect your privacy, and we won't put any of that in the story, but that means that we're going to have to do a shallow interview." I had already flown home, and Billy and I talked about it, and we said we have to respect their professionalism and their profession and honor the interview they actually did, and I'll deal with the fallout. I didn't know it would be twenty-five years of fallout, but it was okay because they wrote a beautiful piece.

L7 DELIBERATELY CHOSE A GENDER-NEUTRAL NAME AND PLAYED down their femininity in order to be taken seriously as a band. This, of course, didn't stop lazy journalists from comparing them to all-female bands like Girlschool, or identifying them as "girls" in reviews, lest a potential listener be shocked upon purchasing the record themselves.

Donita Sparks: Our first record was just titled *L7*. And there was another band in LA called Hardly Dangerous, and they were an all-female band. They were kind of a metal band, you know; they were not from our scene, we were not from their scene. They happened to put out a record that was distributed by the same people that were distributing our record. So the distributor took out a joint ad that said, "Hardly Dangerous and L7, two good reasons to get rock hard." I was working at the *LA Weekly*, and Jonathan Gold, who became a very famous food critic, he was working at the *LA Weekly* at the time, he came up to me, and he said, "Hey, Donita, good to know your distributor isn't sexist." And he shows me that ad, and I just, like [*mimics steam coming out of ears*], bah, like, the steam came out of my ears, because it was just, like, fuck! I deliberately had our name be non–gender specific. Those were conscious decisions. I did not want anything with girls, or any play on words or double entendre, or anything like that. I really wanted it to be like you're just hearing a good rock band, and they might be pleasantly surprised that we're female, you know what I mean? We never wanted to be promoted that way. We refused all-female articles. They would always try to lump us in with, some "Women in Rock" issue—we would refuse. Very early on, we'd do it because we needed some exposure. But once we started to get some momentum, I cut that off. I was like, "We're not doing that."

I felt we deserved our own article that wasn't lumped in with all this other poontang. They always try to do that. That was an issue. Not from other bands, per se; it was an issue with the squares, who were the people who were kind of the media, the suits of whatever stripe, you know. They were the ones who were really hung up on this all-girl thing.

IN 1992, JIM ARUNDEL SPOKE WITH TANYA DONELLY ABOUT HER new band, Belly: "[In Throwing Muses] she was a nervous, skittish platinum blonde then who kept leaving the room to be ill, clutching her stomach. Today, 18 months later, she's a relaxed, jovial brunette who's come to talk about her Belly. Belly is a good earthy name for a group."[4] In Throwing Muses, Tanya was the cute one and Kristin was the crazy one. In Belly, Donelly's move to front person at the height of the alternative revolution meant that she was positioned as the figurehead of her band and as a spokesperson for rock feminism.

Tanya Donelly: Belly didn't feel solo, but it felt like suddenly, even if we were all together, the spotlight was on me. And it felt less like a band than any band I'd been in as a result, even though it was 100 percent a democratic situation. And it was at a time, too, when the focus on women and the onus for one woman to represent all women. And as a result, there was a little bit of a cannibalism that happened where women were kind of turning on each other in the press occasionally. It wasn't completely pervasive, but there were some slings and arrows being thrown, and that leveled me. I could handle almost everything else, except that. I have to say, being challenged on my feminism, on my strength, and how I chose the choices that I made. That microscope coming from other women at the time was just so painful.

Now in hindsight, I'm like, "Oh, that was just sort of more everybody carving space and trying to figure out how we were going to move." It was almost like, "Okay, now there are these voices, and we have to make sure that the voices are saying the right thing to move the agenda forward." And I get that. And I almost agree with it to a certain extent now. Not in a way that I would ever put out there to another woman.

But at the time, I was coming from a place of you write your songs, you play your songs, you tour, you're with your friends. The music was everything, and the songs were everything. And everything else, I naively felt, well, that speaks for itself. I don't have to say anything. Whatever else I do is peripheral to that. It doesn't matter if I don't have pants on in a Gap ad. Which now I would not make that choice. Stuff like that, where I just felt like, "Are you kidding me? After everything that I've done. I'm a music worker." To be questioned because I did one stupid, or several stupid, things. I just sort of feel like in defense of any woman who makes those choices, that's part of the journey. Everyone's trying stuff on all the time. And I feel like that is part of being human and that that shouldn't be questioned and should not have been questioned as vociferously as it was. That was hard.

I navigated most things pretty well. And I figured out how to do interviews, and we figured out as a band who needed to be around us to keep us healthy. And it still felt like Newport, Rhode Island, on the road. For the most part, we weren't surrounded by industry. We weren't surrounded by voices other than our own, for the most part. The hard thing was always the press. And always just sort of how, from our perspective, a fun photo shoot turned into some kind of litmus test as to what we were saying. I wasn't saying anything. I dressed up like Elvis. Who fucking cares? It was just goofy. These light moments took on this weight that was insupportable. Because they're picking who is going to represent the gender, which immediately becomes divisive.

THE MEDIA SITUATED LIZ PHAIR AS THE COUNTERPOINT TO THE androgynous alt-rock norm: a sexy, young, feminine woman who spoke frankly and explicitly about sex. At one point, a record label executive offered her thousands of dollars a month to be his live-in girlfriend. Less obvious consequences included navigating men's expectations without pissing them off or hurting their feelings.

Liz Phair: I feel safer in this industry because of current campaigns of awareness for how unsafe it was in the past and how much sexual harassment, women, especially in the music industry, experienced. God. But it is quaint to laugh and be able to laugh about men being like, "I thought that harassing women was part of the job."

And there is no question that, as a female, I would use men's anticipation of that in the flirting process. I was aware that there was this sense of being friendly and a really chill kind of girl. Whenever I would go do anything, any radio stop, any executive stop, there was this way of having to bejewel men's expectations of some kind of flirty interaction, and then I spent my whole professional life dodging further consequences. It was expected. And to think about that now, it blows in my mind, that you'd have to flirt as a matter of doing business. And then you'd have to figure out how to get out of any expectations that arose from that flirting. We've gotten to the elevator. There'd be this feeling of like, "Okay, I have to get out of here." And it freaked me out that anywhere you went, the guy could be expected to hit on you, and you were supposed to dress in a way that made them think that you were hot. And this was being explicitly said by labels.

LUSCIOUS JACKSON TOURED WITH THE BREEDERS, BUT THEY DIDN'T sound like the Breeders. They didn't really sound like anyone else at all, but they have been referred to as a more somber Breeders rip-off on countless occasions. The band combined harmonies, heavy sampling, keyboard, and R&B grooves with distorted guitar and a steady backbeat. In 1996, they released *Fever In Fever Out* and their first successful single, "Naked Eye." However, Alanis Morissette's *Jagged Little Pill* was released one year earlier, and you couldn't be a woman in a band after that without being compared to her. In his review, Joshua Brown wrote, "These four girls create songs that communicate to the Alanis-worshipping establishment," but if Morissette and Luscious Jackson had male vocalists, this comparison would never have been made. LJ did manage to maintain creative control over almost every aspect of marketing, touring, and recording. The one thing you can't control is what people say about you.

Kate Schellenbach: From the get-go, we were very in charge of our marketing and our imagery. We produced all our albums, coproduced them all. We decided on all our artwork and our photo shoots and clothes and videos. We approved all video concepts and everything about it. Because we were on Grand Royal, the Beastie Boys' record label, they also were doing the same thing. I mean, the Beastie Boys used their advance money to create their own studio and record all their albums themselves. They would make their own videos and direct their own videos. We were using their model of how to succeed in this business and how to keep track. Especially, I think as women, it's super important because we would watch other bands who'd be marketed in this very sexual way. It just worked against them because then they'd play these shows, and people would be yelling, "Take off your shirt and show us your tits!" All that. That didn't happen to us.

We were able to sort of, I guess, give off an image, and maybe you can speak to this better than I, that we were in control and in charge and self-assured, and we weren't having to bare skin in order to sell ourselves. Our first record, there wasn't a picture of us on the cover. I don't think there was a picture of us on the cover until the third record. It was very important for us to sort of maintain that control. There was a time when people were asking us to do magazine fashion shoots and that kind of thing. You'd have these stylists trying to put us in sexy Versace and that kind of stuff. We were just like, "No, sorry, not for us." We were pretty headstrong or naive about the whole thing. Perhaps we would have been that much bigger, but that was just never going to be us. I felt like we were able to deal with our sort of rise in popularity because of that.

Veruca Salt have been accused of a lot of things: of not playing their own instruments, not playing their instruments well enough, of being too attractive, and perhaps the most insulting, of being designed by a marketing focus group.[5]

Louise Post: Following "Seether," Nina and I were thrown in the spotlight, and we weren't necessarily ready for that.

Nina Gordon: Everyone was kind of buzzing about us, and it was all really positive. We felt so much support in Chicago originally. And then all the labels started coming in, and we couldn't believe this was happening and it was happening so fast, and it was flattering, and we were really proud of what we were doing in the studio with Brad; we had no idea how many people were going to hear it. We thought, *Wow, this is really cool. This is really cool and it's really good*, and we were proud of it. So then as soon as things started to take off with *American Thighs*, I think there was a resentment, a backlash. People suggested that we were just some marketing ploy by a major label—by Geffen—we were like some fabricated Menudo-type, Milli Vanilli–type fabrication, which is funny because we were obviously playing our own instruments, and whether we were proficient or super slick, that had nothing to do with it. I think people in Chicago in particular, they kind of eat their own. When things get too big, it's not cool, it's not punk rock, we weren't indie enough, we were too melodic, we were, I don't know—

Louise Post: We were too cute.

Nina Gordon: We were too cute. Well, that was part of it, honestly. It was part of it. Louise got completely skewered for putting on lipstick onstage in London. We played this big show in London, and all the sudden, it was like, "She's not a feminist!"

Louise Post: I was a lipstick feminist.

Nina Gordon: And we felt like we were strongly identified with our feminism, the fact that we were feminists. We felt like we were doing something that we could be completely proud of and should have been proud of, and people were just knocking us down saying, yeah, we were too cute.

Louise Post: Well, and too powerful. It was too much, and so it was the classic like, "These girls are too big for us, and we need to take them down a notch." Ironically, it is what happened to me with Liz Phair, I think both of us—we were blurrily aware of this new name in town, Liz Phair, with this new record and suddenly, she became the hottest thing, the coolest thing to ever happen in Chicago. She was everywhere and we were sort of deluged by press about her and I was kind of over her before I'd even heard her music and ready to dislike it—her having just made *Exile in Guyville* with Brad Wood. Both Nina and I were surprised by how much we loved the record.

I think that happened with us, too. A lot of people heard about us; there was such a mad buzz about us that they just didn't want to like us prior to hearing our music, and then unfortunately, I think the climate then was certainly, "Who are these upstarts? Who do they think they are?"

Nina Gordon: I think for some people it was too poppy, it was too melodic, it was too singsongy or something? People first started talking about our appearance way more than the music. Someone started writing about us, referring to us as "waif rock." They were talking about our body types, and they were talking about our hair. That's what people do. Music is fashion and all that, but there were a few articles that were dismissive and insulting.

MY FAMILY BOUGHT A COMPUTER AND ACQUIRED DIAL-UP INTERnet in 1998. The technology was completely new, and the only part I mastered was the AOL chat feature. I found other young girls obsessed with music and joined a Veruca Salt fan group called the Saltines. We exchanged photos, articles, B-sides, and unreleased tracks on cassette, through the mail, and this is how I got ahold of Liz Phair's Girly-Sound recordings. By this time, I had already formed my first band, recorded an EP at a local studio, and purchased a digital eight-track recorder. My hobbies tend to become obsessions quickly—something I've attributed to my addict brain—and my bandmates didn't share the same drive for celebrity, so when we weren't practicing, I would record my own songs in my room while getting tipsy on Kahlúa and milk. That's what rock stars do. One of the first songs I ever recorded was called "Liz Phair, Marry Me," and surprisingly, Phair was made aware of it in 2021, on the social media site formerly known as Twitter. Apparently, someone, over the course of twenty-four years, stumbled across a burned CD, ripped it to MP3, and uploaded it to a website. I used the opportunity to publicly ask Phair for an interview, and she accepted. Social media is good for something, and that something is marriage proposals.

In the words of Brenda Lee, "You can't always be everyone's darling," a lesson Phair learned as soon as *Exile in Guyville* became a huge success. The broke Chicagoan found her songs being played on New York college radio, which led to a record deal with Matador, and by 1994, she graced the cover of *Rolling Stone* under the headline "A Rock & Roll Star Is Born." According to men—or in Phair's case, the men in Chicago who had encouraged her to pursue songwriting—writing songs for decades in your room doesn't count as "paying your dues." Basically, those Wicker Park guys were jealous because a woman had sidetracked their arbitrary, self-imposed rules and achieved a level of celebrity most of them would never reach. Not only did she pass Go and collect hundreds of dollars, but her album was a "shambling, monotone-voiced, song-by-song response to the Rolling Stones' classic *Exile on Main Street*" that chronicled Chicago's male-dominated alternative-rock scene and basically called them a bunch of know-it-all man babies. Men constantly trashed her. Steve Albini trashed the album publicly, referring to Phair and Smashing Pumpkins as "pandering sluts."*

Liz Phair: The fact that Matador signed me was a signal to everyone to take me seriously, because of Matador's reputation. The fame and the backlash I experienced after *Exile in Guyville* was swift and severe, and I can remember the day that everything changed, because I used to go to this club, the Rainbow, which was the corner local watering house. It was our local bar right there on Damon and Division. And I've been going there for two years. And suddenly, because of one record on Matador and a couple pieces of press, the right kinds of press, people sat

---

*I love Steve Albini. So does Liz Phair, actually.

up and noticed. So I had a number of people whose word other people would take—that it was good stuff—immediately taking my art and moving it forward and moving it up. But the backlash happened so quickly that I could not walk into my local bar the very next day, the very next night, because people were talking about me and arguing about me the minute I walked in. They'd just been discussing me. It had been like, "She's a fucking phony. She's a fraud." And what was I going to say? It had happened overnight. I didn't feel like I totally paid my dues. So what they were saying was true, but right place, right time. What they were discounting was, I don't know, twenty years of education.

The art is the art, business is the business. I was in the right place at the right time. I think when you look at instant fame or instant success, you're always looking at cultural shifts, cultural moments that are much bigger than the individuals. I was prepared. I don't mean to, in any way, take away from my accomplishment. I was competitive, I was trained, and I was hungry. I guess that's competitive.

IN 1993, THE MUSIC INDUSTRY WAS VERY INTO SHOCK VALUE. "My way of doing that was to sort of take agency of my sexuality and just say, like, shocking things in this little girl voice to see if anyone would notice," says Phair.[6] Across genres, the early to mid-'90s was a time when women were asserting control. They were challenging misogyny and insisting their voices be heard. Phair was doing that in a unique way—she was using classic rock as a tool to demystify women and sex. Her frank lyrics lacked the euphemistic ambiguity of pop songs traditionally sung by women. She abandoned flirtation and embraced provocation. Despite the initial fallout, the album remains a '90s alt-rock classic, up there with *Nevermind*, *Live Through This*, and Smashing Pumpkins' *Siamese Dream*, and it single-handedly turned Phair into a national superstar.

LORI BARBERO NOTED A DISMISSIVE COMMENT FROM A FRIEND AND fellow musician following Babes in Toyland's tour with Sonic Youth and major-label signing:

Lori Barbero: In Minnesota, some people liked us and some people didn't like us. One of my best friends said something hurtful once; it was the only hurtful thing he ever said to me. I think it's because maybe he was just a little envious or something because he was a musician, but he said, "Oh, you're just popular because you're girls." And I said, "Really? That's the most stupid thing I've ever heard." Maybe at first it's a novelty and everyone's just like, "You've got to see these wild women." But I'm telling you, I don't think people would come back if it wasn't good. I'm sure there are people that couldn't stand it, but they were curious. But to think that we were only getting the recognition we were getting because we were women. I thought, *That's just dumb*. Either we're liked or we're not liked. It doesn't have anything to do with gender. That's my point of view. And we had to work four times harder than any male band, because men get everything served to them on a silver platter. And we had to prove ourselves time and time and time again. Every time, you have to prove yourself.

IN 1998, I SHARED A ROOM WITH MY SISTER. IT WAS ON THE SECond floor of a tiny Cape and had slanted ceilings and no door.

This is important because my vividest memories of this room are contained to the découpage mess I made of my walls. I studiously pored over magazines, cut out glossy photos of my favorite bands, and glued them to my wall until it was completely covered. I remember being bothered that women in rock didn't seem prevalent in the poster bins at Strawberries or Sam Goody. Only Nirvana and Pearl Jam gained space amid the Grateful Dead and shirtless Jim Morrisons. Garbage released *Version 2.0* in 1998, and *Rolling Stone* dubbed it "the only pop-rock album that matters so far." Shirley Manson had become the spokesperson for the band and an entire generation of young women. What I didn't know until we spoke in 2018 was that Manson wasn't always the focal point of Garbage. In 1995, she wasn't who journalists wanted to speak to; it was Butch, the producer behind Nirvana and Smashing Pumpkins. She had to overcome several hurdles as a woman in a band, as a woman in a band with three established men, and as a young woman in a band with much older, male musicians.

Shirley Manson: In Garbage, I felt like I was perceived as this dummy, lucky little bunny who came along and fluffed everything and made it look a little prettier. Well, there was a multitude of things going on. One, I felt that I wasn't as talented as my band. Two, I certainly wasn't as respected and probably never would be. And three, I felt dominated. So there was a lot of things going on. That changed very quickly, but certainly at the beginning, even the people that we worked with at the record label were always sort of saying, "We're going to try and get her press, but they're only going to want to talk to you, Butch." And that was what was presented to me right at the beginning. And I was a little intimidated by that because it immediately made me feel like, "Well, I'm not doing my job. I'm not good at my job, and I'm not doing my job."

And as I said, that very, very quickly changed, thank God. Because otherwise, I don't think the band would have ever worked if I hadn't been as dominant as I am. And I'm a pretty dominant, articulate, and up-front individual. So I managed to save myself in the end. But I think if I'd been a more gentle, more reticent female, I probably would have been drowned out. And therefore, if you don't have a strong figurehead in a band, you're going to get totally steamrolled over by any other bands who are around at the time. You have to stand out. You need to have a good peacock, and I was an effective peacock.

Because we had Butch, who was this respected producer, we were left alone in the studio; we basically just did our own thing and delivered the records, and that was the end of it. We were the zeitgeist, en vogue band, and I was the it girl. I mean, the number of opportunities that came our way were ridiculous. The amount of front covers I got were almost bordering on embarrassing to the point where I remember getting very self-conscious and felt like, "I'm being overexposed here. This is not good."

IN 1992, DONITA SPARKS DROPPED HER PANTS DURING A LIVE PER-formance on *The Word*, blasting her pixelated bits and butt cheeks into UK homes. People debated whether it was a feminist statement or pure provocation without considering whether it could be both. British music magazine *NME* eviscerated Sparks not because she dropped her pants but because she didn't do it the way Madonna did. It wasn't sexy. Women in rock were praised in the press for their feminism but were also constantly judged against impossible standards and according to imaginary perceptions of feminist perfection.

Donita Sparks: We were playing a live television show, and there had just been a parade of men walking around in banana hammocks with their asses out. First of all, I love absurdity. I was in a surreal situation, and I used to do performance art in the '80s, so I went performance art on their ass and dropped my pants on live television. And I threw my tampon into the crowd at the Reading Festival. That's a little bit John Waters, too, you know—it was an act that had many influences. It was feminist, it was performance art. It was John Waters. It was defiant and funny and feminist all at the same time.

MAINSTREAM MEDIA COVERAGE WAS BOTH A RISK AND AN OPPOR-tunity whose consequences were difficult to foresee. On the one hand, the media was clearly excited by the prospect of an army of angry women. Despite their deliberate rejection of conventional expectations about female beauty, women in various states of wild abandon and undress were bound to prove titillating for the readers of Middle America. On the other hand, this alternative phenomenon had the ingredients for moral panic. There was sex, violence, substance abuse, and political activism. There was revolutionary rhetoric and discussion of hot topics such as rape and misogyny that were beginning to appear on the media radar and echoed by male bands. Media editors saw this as an opportunity to reach elusive younger readers.

Inevitably, there was a fair amount of inaccuracy and misrepresentation to be found in such coverage. Quotations were taken out of context, nuances were ignored, and much of the analysis was superficial. Journalists were inclined to speak to participants who were ready and willing to speak to them; and in the process, they portrayed a few figureheads as representative of an entire culture. They conflated riot grrrl with distinct musical scenes, and artists like L7, Hole, and Babes in Toyland have been lumped, inaccurately, into the riot grrrl category. They oversimplified—and sometimes mocked—revolutionary feminist politics. They exaggerated, trivialized, and sensationalized. They perpetuated the scarcity myth, that there is only room for one or two women at a time, and pitted women against one another.

By mid-1993, *Rolling Stone* was already announcing that riot grrrls were "at war" with other female rock performers—creating the spectacle of a catfight. Courtney Love and Kim Gordon of Sonic Youth were both quoted criticizing Kathleen Hanna and Bikini Kill for being "sanctimonious" and "setting a new yardstick" by which female performers were to be measured. The rivalry culminated when Love punched Hanna in the face at a rock festival in 1995: she was convicted and sent to anger-management classes. The differences here were not just personal but explicitly political. Hanna resented being aligned with other female bands outside the immediate riot grrrl scene. She described Love as "assimilationist" (in *Option* magazine, 1992), and clearly saw herself as more militantly feminist. Yet even Hanna could not entirely evade the lure of celebrity feminism: in 1994, for example, she was profiled in *Ms.* magazine in a feature on "50 Ways to be a Feminist," complete with a picture showing the word *SLUT* on her bare midriff, and she maintains her position as the singular figurehead of the riot grrrl movement.[7]

What's happened retrospectively is that any loud, abrasive women have been relabeled riot grrrl. And it's not just the laypeople or uneducated music fans on Spotify—people who curate riot grrrl playlists with Hole, Meredith Brooks (she wrote that song "Bitch" about being a bitch), L7, Veruca Salt, and even twenty-first-century bands like the Gossip and Yeah Yeah Yeahs—it's journalists. People who are gainfully employed in the field of music writing. In 2018, I curated a sold-out event in Los Angeles featuring an intergenerational lineup of artists like Alice Bag, Julie Cafritz, Patty Schemel, Alice de Buhr of Fanny, the late, great Kat Arthur, and Allison Wolfe of Bratmobile. I'm a total scrapper and pulled this off with friends, so I was pleasantly surprised that we got a lot of press—even Kim Gordon showed up! But 90 percent of the time, the event was covered as riot grrrl despite having only one riot grrrl in attendance. Women-centered punk, grunge, rock, and alternative music, if you were outspoken or feminist, you've been recuperated by mainstream media as riot grrrl. This is ahistorical and lazy journalism. But it is also the consequence of music criticism from the '90s that utilized critical maneuvers like rhetorical containment (i.e., lumping all "women in rock" into a single category).[8]

Donita Sparks: I think that to people who don't know what the riot grrrl movement or the grunge phenomenon was could misconstrue L7 as an archetype of riot grrrl or a grunge band. I'm the one who threw the tampon, our audiences were literally riots—stage-diving mayhem. We dressed very grungy, our hair was matted, dirty, dreaded, and clumped, and our clothes were torn. None of us knew how to sew, and we would duct-tape our pants closed. For people who don't know what riot grrrl was, that it came from a college campus, or that we were a working-class band from LA, not Seattle—I think that could be confusing.

THE DOMINANT CULTURE WITHIN ROCK JOURNALISM CAN AFFECT what is—and more importantly what cannot be—written.[9] This stems from overarching societal norms and affects readers' perceptions. Women are not considered capable of producing serious music, usually because the assumptions surrounding what serious music comprises—particularly in regard to the issue of credibility—are constructed by a capitalist, patriarchal music press in a manner that systematically excludes women by valuing masculinity and devaluing femininity.[10] Although the press must include women to appear liberal and nonsexist, they describe women in rock as a new phenomenon that is periodically discovered. This can occur because retrospective writing on "serious" popular music excludes the women who may have been at the forefront of any given movement, but it might also be that rock writers and critics are sexist. The "exclusion of women from history" means they are a perpetual novelty, and each new group of successful female performers is heralded as the first.[11] As a result of their gendered and anomalous representation, they are consequently excluded from the history, the canon, and the cycle is doomed to repeat itself. The way the press treated women in rock in the 1990s made it easier to disappear them once the cultural tide began to turn. In this way, it makes women in rock expendable, nifty little trinkets and novelties that show up occasionally, ultimately ostracizing them from historical memory.

Chapter 4

BEFORE WE KNEW IT, WE WERE TOPPING THE CHARTS

Our ambitions were to just be a good alternative
band that had a modest career. And then before
we knew it, we were topping the charts.

—Shirley Manson, Garbage

FOLLOWING THE HOTLY CONTESTED SENATE CONFIRMATION
hearings for Supreme Court nominee and all-around hypo-
critical piece of shit Clarence Thomas, 1992 was labeled "Year
of the Woman." It was a banner year for female candidates, with
11 women winning party nominations for the US Senate, and
108 for the House of Representatives. A similar wave of women

was elected in the 2018 House elections following the election of Donald Trump and the Brett Kavanaugh confirmation hearings; unfortunately, that dystopian turn of events did not have the same impact on mainstream pop and rock music, whereas the early '90s witnessed an exaltation of antiestablishment, alt-rock women.

Sonic Youth had already released six albums on SST and Enigma Records before breaking all the cool-kid rules and signing to DGC in 1990. *Goo* became the band's major-label debut, but its release represented a kind of do-over after the distribution problems the group ran into with Enigma Records—an independent label with major-label distribution—and their 1988 album *Daydream Nation*. After spending $30,000 on that album and not seeing commercial performance match up to its critical acclaim, Sonic Youth made a deal with Geffen Records that would last for more than two decades. The album, though still rife with the band's noise-ridden freak-outs and buzzy dirges, saw them making the most of their newfound resources, with tracks like "Kool Thing," featuring a guest appearance from Chuck D, predicting the grunge explosion ever so slightly too early.[1] Nirvana followed suit and signed with DGC, as did Hole, Veruca Salt, the Raincoats, and That Dog. The band released a documentary called *1991: The Year Punk Broke* before it did. The film follows Sonic Youth on tour and showcases Nirvana, Babes in Toyland, Gumball, Dinosaur Jr., and the Ramones.

But 1993–95 might be alternative rock's "Years of the Women." A tsunami of rock women released albums on major labels, to critical acclaim. In '93, The Breeders released *Last Splash* on 4AD/Elektra; Belly unleashed their debut album, *Star*, on Sire/Reprise in the US; Liz Phair released *Exile in Guyville* on Matador Records; Mazzy Star's second studio album, *So Tonight That*

I Might See, was released on Capitol Records; the Juliana Hatfield Three released *Become What You Are* on Mammoth Records, and the single "Spin the Bottle" was featured in the film *Reality Bites*. The alternative phenomenon had a global reach as well: London's Elastica released their hit single "Stutter" on DGC. Island Records released the Cranberries debut and PJ Harvey's second album, *Rid of Me*. In 1994, Hole's seminal album *Live Through This* was unleashed onto the masses four days after Kurt Cobain's body was discovered. Veruca Salt's *American Thighs* came out on Minty Fresh / DGC, and L7's fourth studio album, *Hungry for Stink*, was released on Slash/Reprise. The Cranberries and Liz Phair released sophomore albums, *No Need to Argue* and *Whip-Smart*. And finally, in 1995, Garbage unveiled their debut album; Alanis Morissette shocked mainstream audiences with her third album, *Jagged Little Pill*; PJ Harvey released *To Bring You My Love*; and Elastica finally finished their self-titled debut.

University is the 1995 album by Throwing Muses, released on Sire/Reprise in the US and on 4AD elsewhere. The single "Bright Yellow Gun" became the band's first national hit. I bought a pair of Doc Martens boots the same year and was gifted a CD featuring "Bright Yellow Gun" and the Breeders single "Safari." The album's radio exposure led to feature articles in *Rolling Stone* and other major music magazines. The album was recorded in the fall of 1993, right before lead Muse Kristin Hersh recorded her first solo album, *Hips and Makers*. 4AD founder and president Ivo Watts-Russell convinced Hersh to release the solo album first, in early 1994. This led to *University* being delayed until 1995. Despite all the acclaim and exposure for the album, sales were disappointingly low (by major-label standards), and the band was dropped from Sire's roster, ending the Muses' major-label years.

Kristin Hersh: When Tanya left, Throwing Muses recorded *Red Heaven* (1992) as a trio with our original bass player, Leslie Langston, and it was just what we felt like doing. And Warner Bros. sort of got it. "Oh! She's the one that likes to make noise and she looks like a normal person," and they just sort of forgave me. And oddly, Leslie only did the record; we hired our bass player who's still in the band, who has been in my band now for twenty-something years, Bernard Georges. He's done the tour, and he's done every record since. The next record we made was our biggest record ever, which didn't make any sense at all. We didn't care, but what we did care about was the music, and that came across, and alternative music was then big.

We were on the radio, and they let us make our own video. I had one of my friends from RISD [Rhode Island School of Design] make a video with chimps. We called PETA and said, "Give us a chimp wrangler that you think is okay," and Dave and Bernie played pimps, I think? Warner Bros. were letting us do anything we wanted, and they just couldn't believe that this alternative thing that we had brought to them was now big, but they just couldn't handle the drag queens and the drinking, and the chimp and I go to bed together; we trash the hotel room and smoke cigarettes, and they just hated the smoking. So they gave us another budget—like $100k or something—to make a different video, and we're like, "Can we just keep it?"

They got the guy who made a Nirvana video to do the "real" "Bright Yellow Gun" video, and it was us in a room they built inside a soundstage in Los Angeles. While we played, a camera was dropped down by a cable, and we would just push it around, so it was just shooting us kind of in the round. While it happened, they filled the room with water, and it didn't occur to anyone—you know, electricity, water, and drowning. We couldn't get out of there until midnight, and the water level was rising.

Later, Warner Bros. wouldn't work to sell our records. They used us to sign young bands who were fans of ours, but they wouldn't lift a finger to help our careers. And they were their records, you'd think they'd want to sell them, but they chose three or four to work, the ones that are going to fly, meaning the dumb ones, and they don't do anything else, and they still get their paychecks. So they'd let me into their offices to ask why they sold crap, and they'd say, "Because crap sells." It's like, "That's because you sell crap." They hadn't investigated the untapped audience of intelligent music listeners. Musically literate people demand substance over style, and all they were doing was marketing style, throwing it away, and marketing another style, throwing it away. It was just fashion sound, and so we extricated ourselves. I bought us off Warner Bros. by giving them my first solo record, *Hips and Makers*.

WHEN GRUNGE "HAPPENED," MAJOR-LABEL REPRESENTATIVES traveled the country, scouted for promising bands at festivals, and sometimes ignited vicious bidding wars for "the next big thing." Alt-rock women were marketable and worth investing in, and in turn, many found themselves thrust into the corporate music business. The benefits included major-label distribution, which meant global recognition. It also meant a salary. Not necessarily pocket money but huge recording and video advances (like millions of dollars) and tour support.

Donita Sparks: *Bricks Are Heavy* came out in '92, and that was, like, worldwide, you know? We had representation in Japan, South America, everywhere. So that's when it really kind of blew open.

Lori Barbero: We toured constantly for probably twenty-plus years, so we missed tons and tons of music. If we didn't do a festival with them or tour with them or cross paths with them on tour, I probably wasn't really exposed to them, because it was before cell phones. It was before GPS. I mean, I had paper maps and I had to stop at truck stops before the shows and find a hotel. There was a lot on our plate. It wasn't that we were just being ignorant. We did Lollapalooza, played with Alice in Chains, Tool, and Dinosaur Jr.; we did a huge tour with My Bloody Valentine. We toured with White Zombie. I mean, we were just spun. We were three Tasmanian devils going around wherever we were booked, Europe or Japan or Australia, the United States, doing what we did—and the only thing we knew how to do.

We had a manager, Richard Bishop, and he'd be like, "Oh, you should bring this band on tour." And we would go, "No, we're going to bring this band on tour." I don't give a rat's ass if they're getting big. We don't know them. We might not really care for them, and we're going to bring someone on tour with us that we like and we want to help because someone did that for us. My thing is, I've always been kind of weird about tour band managers that have never been in a band. I just think if you've never been in a band, how can you relate? They're on the business side, looking at it with dollar signs. We're looking at it as a career. Sure, money's great, but our passion is greater than money, and it doesn't make any difference to us. We'll sleep on people's floors for three years if we get to tour with the bands that we love. Of course we want to get paid, but the passion is part of the job.

I worked with Minor Threat back in '82. I brought them to the Twin Cities. I used to put together a lot of concerts, too, before there were all-ages shows. I learned a lot from them, too: they never had any merchandise, they toured in a van, and they were just this punk rock aesthetic, just like Sonic Youth. *Worship* is a strong word, but it's the only word I can think of. I worship their aesthetics. I worship how Sonic Youth could have done whatever, but what you see is what you get. They worked really hard, and they didn't change because someone else thought they needed to. They just did what they wanted to, and they followed their heartstrings instead of their wallets or what people thought they should do.

Tanya Donelly: Once Belly happened, I re-signed with Warner Bros. on the heels of *Star.* We signed it after the record had already taken off. It was when my contract came up, so that was a fortuitous moment. But again, if you wanted to really be making a living, you had to tour all the time. There was an eighteen-month tour at one point when I was in Belly, just to make sure that we were in the black at the end of it.

Louise Post: We had been on tour opening for Live and playing these big sheds all summer long. Their sound person rung out the system every day during sound check to "Enter Sandman" [by Metallica] so we heard that song every day while sitting at catering outside somewhere, eating lunch, and every day, we're like, "Goddamn, this sounds good." One day, someone said, "What if we recorded with Bob Rock?" At that time, we also had Metallica's management, so it was an easy introduction. While we were recording *Eight Arms to Hold You* with him—we laugh about this now—but we said, "When did we go from grunge to glam?" It could have been a Tuesday.

Nina Gordon: Part of the whole "women in rock" thing is, and I assume that this must happen to guys on some level, but you spend so much of your time sitting in a chair, getting your makeup done and having your hair done and looking at your face and criticizing every little detail. We enjoyed the glamorous aspect of it. It's fun to see yourself all made up and wearing great clothes! It's fun playing dress-up and doing all that stuff, but there's also a darker side—which is you spend more time focusing on that and less time on the music. You get insular and narcissistic, and there is that aspect of being a quote-unquote rock star, where you start feeling powerful; you've got other people taking care of you, you've got people doing everything for you. [You] would show up at airports, a car would come pick you up, bring you to an airport, you don't know anything about the flight you're on or where you're going. You just show up and somebody is bringing your meals, and all this stuff is happening and you lose touch with reality. We didn't have people who grounded us. We had managers who would admit themselves [that they] didn't really understand women. We had tour managers that were addicts and totally out of control themselves.

Our record label wouldn't have let us break up if we were as big as the Rolling Stones or something. If you are that, then everybody fights to keep you together, but in our situation, our second record didn't meet the expectations that everybody had for it. It did incredibly well in the grand scheme of things, but when push came to shove, and when everything started to fall apart, they all let it fall apart.

Melissa Auf der Maur: When I joined Hole, I was paid $600 a week, and I was a bass player. And then suddenly, they went from the old Kurt [Cobain] management to Q Prime, this massive, insane Def Leppard, Metallica management. They're pretty legendary.

I signed a five-year contract, and all these crazy things happened. We toured *Live Through This* forever. *Celebrity Skin* took forever to write and record, and there was some hope in that it was a weird, polished, corporate record, but there had been no other female voices on radio other than Gwen Stefani and Alanis Morissette in 1996. It was like, "This is a big deal that Courtney's voice is the only other woman on mainstream rock radio." And that was kind of enough to be like, "Well, maybe there was a point to this insane overly produced record." I was watching in total horror and disgust as management spent a million dollars on a music video. They were trying to make Courtney into a Top 40 thing, and I thought they'd all lost their minds. I just really disconnected myself from so much of that. But I was at every single writing session.

We released *Celebrity Skin* in '98 and played an amazing show at Glastonbury in '99. We did a couple of headlining festivals in Australia and Canada where we were the only women, as always. We're always the only women on the bill, and we're the headliners. It was a huge deal, and I was so proud of it. And I was satisfied even though it had been tumultuous and difficult. Courtney and I were getting along better than we ever had. She was really, like, quite sober and together, and suddenly, her movie career started taking off and I had a sense like, "Uh-oh. She's not going to support this record, because she's going to want to make another movie," and I didn't want to be in a band that didn't work.

GARBAGE'S DEBUT STUDIO ALBUM WAS MET WITH COMMERCIAL AND critical acclaim and viewed by some as an innovative recording for its time. It reached #20 on the US Billboard 200 and #6 on the

Official UK Albums Chart, while charting inside the top twenty and receiving multiplatinum certifications in several territories. The band promoted the album on a yearlong tour, including playing on the European festival circuit and supporting Smashing Pumpkins throughout 1996, as well as by a run of increasingly successful singles culminating with "Stupid Girl," which received Grammy Award nominations for Best Rock Song and Best Rock Performance by a Duo or Group in 1997.

Shirley Manson: The fame was intense. It was unexpected—uninvited, really, in a way. I had never, ever chased after the kind of success I've enjoyed. I can remember saying to somebody once, "If I could just be as big as Echo & the Bunnymen, I would be so happy. It would be the coolest, it would just be the coolest." And our ambitions were to just be a good alternative band that had a modest career. And then before we knew it, we were topping charts. I mean, it was crazy.

Garbage got an opportunity to give a track to—at the time what was considered very hip—this CD magazine called *Volume*, which came out of the UK. And it had all this sort of like upcoming new bands, and we got invited to give a track to *Volume*. We gave "Vow," as it turns out, which was our first single. But the only reason we gave that track out was because it was the only one even remotely close to being finished. So we put it out on *Volume*, and it got an extraordinary response out of the UK and out of Australia. And they started playing it on the radio.

And suddenly, record labels started biting and wanting to sign us and getting very excited. Things were starting to boil on the press, and we could feel it ourselves. Even though we were in the Midwest, in Madison, Wisconsin, the middle of nowhere, completely isolated from the industry, we began to feel it. And I think

Liz Phair at Prospect Park, June 29, 2019 (*Photo credit: Edwina Hay*)

Liz Phair at Prospect Park, June 29, 2019 (*Photo credit: Edwina Hay*)

Donita Sparks (L7) at Warsaw in Brooklyn, New York, in 2022 (*Photo credit: Edwina Hay*)

Kat Bjelland (Babes in Toyland) at Irving Plaza in 2015 (*Photo credit: Edwina Hay*)

Peaches and Shirley Manson (Garbage) at Amsterjam at Randall's Island on August 20, 2005 (*Photo credit: Edwina Hay*)

Josephine Wiggs (The Breeders) in "4AD's 13 Year Itch" at ICA Theatre in London, 1993 (*Photo credit: Brad Searles*)

Kim Deal (The Breeders) in "4AD's 13 Year Itch" at ICA Theatre in London, 1993 (*Photo credit: Brad Searles*)

Kristin Hersh (Throwing Muses) in "4AD's 13 Year Itch" at ICA Theatre in London, 1993 (*Photo credit: Brad Searles*)

Tanya Donelly and Kristin Hersh (Throwing Muses) at the Sinclair in Boston, Massachusetts, in 2014 (*Photo credit: Brad Searles*)

Liz Phair and Brad Wood on the UK tour in 1993 *(Photo credit: Brad Wood)*

Liz Phair and Brad Wood on the UK tour in 1993 *(Photo credit: Brad Wood)*

Polaroid of Liz Phair, Brad Wood, and Casey Rice *(Photo credit: Brad Wood)*

Nina Gordon and Louise Post (Veruca Salt) in 1997 *(Photo credit: Louise Post)*

Louise Post, Steve Lack, and Nina Gordon in 1995 *(Photo credit: Louise Post)*

Louise Post and Nina Gordon backstage in 1998 *(Photo credit: Louise Post)*

Donita Sparks (L7) at Club Babyhead in Providence, Rhode Island, on March 29, 1992 (*Photo credit: Denise Monahan-Murphy*)

Donita Sparks and Jennifer Finch (L7) (*Photo credit: Denise Monahan-Murphy*)

Jill Emery (Hole) at the Rathskeller in Boston on November 7, 1991 (*Photo credit: Denise Monahan-Murphy*)

Courtney Love (Hole) at the Rathskeller in Boston, Massachusetts, on November 7, 1991 (*Photo credit: Denise Monahan-Murphy*)

Courtney Love (*Photo credit: Denise Monahan-Murphy*)

Courtney Love (Hole) at the Rathskeller in Boston on November 7, 1991 (*Photo credit: Denise Monahan-Murphy*)

Lori Barbero (Babes in Toyland) at the Middle East in Cambridge, Massachusetts, in 1993 (*Photo credit: Denise Monahan-Murphy*)

Kat Bjelland (Babes in Toyland) (*Photo credit: Denise Monahan-Murphy*)

Throwing Muses live in Providence, Rhode Island, in 1988 (*Photo credit: Tanya Donelly*)

Throwing Muses backstage in 1988 (*Photo credit: Tanya Donelly*)

Belly in 1995 (*Photo credit: Tanya Donelly*)

Belly with Conan O'Brien (*Photo credit: Tanya Donelly*)

On the bus (*Photo credit: Tracy Bonham*)

Tracy Bonham live at Mama Kin in Boston, Massachusetts, in 1996 (*Photo credit: Tracy Bonham*)

Selene Vigil (7 Year Bitch) at T. T. the Bear's Place in Cambridge, Massachusetts, in 1996 (*Photo credit: Melissa Leclerc*)

Elizabeth Davis (7 Year Bitch) at T. T. the Bear's Place in Cambridge, Massachusetts, in 1996 (*Photo credit: Melissa Leclerc*)

Calendar (7 Year Bitch) at T. T. the Bear's Place in Cambridge, Massachusetts, in 1996 (*Photo credit: Melissa Leclerc*)

Kat Bjelland (Babes in Toyland) at Ziggy's in Winston-Salem, North Carolina, on October 28, 1995 (*Photo credit: Courtney Brooke*)

Maureen Herman (Babes in Toyland) at Ziggy's in Winston-Salem,
North Carolina, in 1997 (*Photo credit: Courtney Brooke*)

Gail Greenwood (*Photo credit: Courtney Brooke*)

we all started to go, "Oh my God! This could actually be a reality in the end." But it was unexpected. And it was like wildfire. It just ignited. And then before we knew it, it had grown into a fire, and record labels were falling over themselves to come and sign us, and it was exciting.

The thing that I don't think people quite understand about that trajectory for us was, that whole period in the '90s was the first time alternative music (i.e., anyone who was non-conformist) suddenly became the popular kid. Suddenly, we were overtaking everything. If you weren't alternative, you weren't getting played on MTV, you weren't getting played on the radio, you weren't getting on the front covers of music magazines. So it was a surprise for everyone. And this mad movement that began arguably as sort of grunge and then exploded and disappeared in a puff of air when September 11 occurred. But there was that much trajectory for a moment.

We weren't on a major label when we first came out. We signed to an independent label called Mushroom Records in the UK and out of Australia. And we also signed to independent here in the US, Almo Records, which was the next incarnation of A&M Records. So, we were very independent right from the start, and from that point of view, we were very lucky. We were not in the major-label system for the first two records. And because the trajectory of our career was so incredible for the first two records, we were left to our own devices, pretty much.

Because we had Butch [Vig], who was this respected producer, we were left alone in the studio; we basically just did our own thing, delivered the records, and that was the end of it. The workload was insane. But I take a lot of responsibility for that because I made my band work. I knew how difficult it was out there. I had come from a touring band; they hadn't. And I was like, "We need

to work. If we want to stick around, we're going to have to work."
You have to connect with people. If you don't connect with people, they're on to the next person about two seconds later. Sometimes we'd be playing two gigs a day on very little sleep, and we
were kind of exhausted. I don't regret a minute of it. I mean, I'm
so grateful that we had the energy and the willingness to put in
that kind of work. Because it's paid off in spades for twenty-two
years at this point.

Kate Schellenbach: In 1995, we opened for R.E.M. for months.
We toured with that band Live. We did our own headlining
tours, too. We brought the Lunachicks on tour with us. It's the
typical rock and roll story: we started in a van, worked our way
up to an RV, and eventually, we were in a tour bus. It was nice. It
was fun. Then we put out one EP and three full-length albums
on Capitol Records.

Our second album was the one that had the song "Naked Eye"
on it, which was an early song that we charted with. By that
time, we were touring; we were able to pay ourselves a salary.
We ultimately are still in debt to our publishing company and
all that stuff, but we were making enough money on tour, selling
merchandise, and with publishing advances to pay ourselves a
nice salary. But we weren't living large or anything. We all still
lived in our shitty little apartments in New York and that kind
of thing. But there was a point we had a few side musicians touring with us. At some point, we were like, "They're making more
money than we are because we're paying them salaries and the
per diem and all that stuff." Basically, you have to sell a million
records in order to make money off of that. We weren't a band
that would tour for a year. We'd tour for a month and then take
some time to regroup and then tour. We weren't road dogs. I

think that it works against you trying to make a living because you sell merchandise, and that's a way to make money.

But the third album was when we charted. Even that was, like, I don't know. Maybe it was #24 on the Hot 100. I don't even know. We never got a number. We weren't huge, huge, huge, where it was unbearable. Then we also made sure to try to pick tours and strategize about where we were playing and having days off just to maintain sort of mental health, which is really hard. Anybody who tours will tell you, like, being on the road, you can understand why everyone becomes drunks and drug addicts. You're tired, you're hungry, you're not where you want to be. Someone else is in control of every aspect of your comfort and your well-being. There's just that hour, hour and a half a day where you're doing your job, and the rest of the time, you're just sort of like waiting around. We tried to have as much fun as we could and stay creative.

I think the '90s were great. I think being connected to the Beastie Boys was a blessing and being on their label and having allies that understood where we were coming from. We toured with them, which was not great, because anybody who opens for the Beastie Boys, it's a horrible slot to be in because nobody wants to see anybody but the Beastie Boys. But it was really fun.

Josephine Wiggs: Luscious Jackson supported us in Europe. There was a woman who was working at the LA office of 4AD who told me about Luscious Jackson. She had seen them play and they were really good, and then someone gave Kim [Deal] a cassette of their first record, *In Search of Manny*. So they came over and did the European tour with us. *Last Splash* had come out; we had a tour bus and catering. We took catering with us on the road. It was fantastic. You would arrive after an overnight drive and there was breakfast. There was a hot meal waiting for you. It was so comforting and lovely. It really was. And Luscious Jackson got tour support from Capitol Records because they also were in on the catering thing. We blew all the money we ever would have made on that one tour by having catering. And I think we took a monitor system around with us, too. Monitoring. We spent all the money right there and then never made another penny since.

Zia McCabe: There were so many employees at Capitol. And I remember my take on it was, these guys are working for a ton of bands, right? And they've got a roster, and they're making cold calls, especially like college radio, are making these phone calls for all these bands. And there's no way they're all getting treated totally equal. So, my thing was forging these relationships with these people so that there was a real person that you were working for, not a band on a list. And that was my contribution. That's how I felt like I could make a difference. I'd show up in my roller skates and blowing bubbles and, you know, bikini; it was so fun. And I felt like it worked. I felt like we were extending our community to these major-label people. People who maybe don't always feel in community with the musicians that they work with. Unfortunately, every album was a completely different staff. And so, everyone was just gone, and I'm like, "Where's all the friends I made?" When it's always different people, it doesn't feel as genuine. Now I'm like glad-handing to get these people to remember me. It lost its authenticity. And I lost the steam of starting over by the third time. I just didn't care. And I could tell that they didn't really either. We'd already had a couple albums out. We didn't blow up the way that they thought we were going to. And we were pretty defiant.

I HAVE THIS VIVIDLY AWKWARD MEMORY OF MY MOM BRINGING MY grandmother down to my basement room while I was practicing guitar (I was always practicing). It was 1997, and I was obsessed with Tracy Bonham's debut. It was the only record of hers I owned until I sat down with her for an interview in 2017 and discovered, to my surprise, that she never stopped working. Bonham had the fortune of being plucked out of the Boston music scene during a pretty pivotal moment for women in the industry. The downside is that she was plucked at the tail end of that era and robbed of the opportunity to build a visible catalog. I played "Sharks Can't Sleep" for my grandma, who seemed supportive at first but ultimately unimpressed, a fitting metaphor for Bonham's experience with the major-label system.

Tracy Bonham: I had a manager who was kind of a massage-a-little-bit, kind of old-school manager, came from that world of music, is like, "Hey, listen, baby." That kind of thing. And a lot of the people that were at the record label had that as well. And I could play the role of, like, the cute little sister and not have to say anything, but I think that's what started this kind of dynamic where I kind of set things up to fail.

I didn't realize it at the time. I would go out on tour, and I didn't know how to say no, honestly, so they ran me ragged. So I went out on a couple of tours at the beginning, and that was pretty fun. We were in like a really cool van and all that stuff. But then when things started to get serious and I had a hit, they booked me and booked me and booked me, and it was like tour bus after tour bus, which, I'm not complaining. Because that was exciting, but it was hard work. There was no free time. And I didn't know how to say, "Wait, stop." Or even if it was something as small as like the scheduling through the day of like, "Okay, you're going to interviews in the morning and then going to have breakfast and interviews, and then you sign posters during your lunch," and that gets to you after a while. And if you don't know how to say *stop*, or if you don't have a manager who's really looking out for your best interest—he's just kind of like not honking the horn, because he didn't give a shit.

And he had me, probably even said, "There's no crying in rock and roll," at one point. I remember that that was really, really hard, and it started to eat away at me. So, I spent ten months on the road when I had the hit with "Mother Mother." It was nonstop with maybe a few days at home. I missed my grandfather's funeral. You miss things in life, and that starts to bother you, too, but you're on this machine and you're like, "No, I have to keep going." And everybody's expecting this from me, and they're always dangling the carrot. It's kind of ubiquitous.

It's not like anyone intended this, but, for instance, if you don't go on *The Howard Stern Show*, then maybe you might not get those other followers. So, everyone was like, "If you do that, maybe you'll get that." There's always that lure. And there were times when I think my biological clock was clicked; the clock was ticking a little bit, even though I was like late twenties. I would hear like the cry of a baby in the next room, and I'd be like, "Oh!" and then quickly got that out of my mind. There was no time for that.

It was very confusing. I had a lot of guilt because I let some friends down; I didn't go to somebody's wedding. Those are the hard parts of living in a bubble on a tour bus and everybody's taking care of you, and I've got business managers now, too. So I haven't like written a check in a long time and that's awesome, but it's not the real world. It's very like pampered and strange. I also didn't really enjoy the brief brush with fame as much as other people might have. It made me very insecure, and I felt very self-conscious everywhere I went.

It's not as fun as they make it seem. It's not that glamorous. You're not really like out seeing the sights; you might get a day off in Vienna or something, but it's lonely. And I wasn't really a band either, so there was confusion and conflict. I'm a singer-songwriter. I want these guys to feel like they're in my band, and I want to hang out and have this kind of altruistic thing going on, but it's really my band. There was a lot of tension between me and my musicians because they were kind of resentful of that. And that didn't make it easy either. It was very lonely.

I was nominated for these two Grammys in 1997, and I did not win. And I kind of feel like that was a moment where it could have gone this way or it could have gone that way. And because I didn't, I lost the support from the label.

Melissa Auf der Maur: I can't say that anybody in the band was good with business. And I do feel very bad because in the end, I don't think it worked out well. Nineteen ninety-seven was like the last dying breath of the corporate minions destroying alternative culture. So it was just like the last moment of corporatizing every drop of alternative culture.

CELEBRITY SKIN IS A POP RECORD AND A DRASTIC DEVIATION FROM its predecessor, *Live Through This.* Producer Michael Beinhorn glossed it up and recommended that the band replace Patty Schemel with a session musician Patty refers to as "Johnny One-Take" in her memoir, *Hit So Hard.* Patty appears on the album cover but left the band and was replaced by touring drummer Samantha Maloney.

Patty Schemel: I used Johnny One-Take as an excuse to just go out and get high and disappear. There's always that "Oh, I wish I would have done things differently," but the way I reacted to that whole thing was exactly the way I was supposed to. I was able to just drift out into, you know, crack heroin island, and stay there for a long time, because first of all, that's the way I dealt with any difficulties, and secondly, because my identity was that I was the drummer of Hole. And at the time, I thought, *That's it, there's nothing else.* Now I know of course there's so much more to me than that. And I guess I could say that I had that experience, and every path takes you to where you need to go, so I figured out what's important. And if I didn't do it that way, I wouldn't have figured it out. If I didn't lose it all, I wouldn't have figured out that I like—cooking or whatever.

Melissa Auf der Maur: I had a great time working on that record. I just stayed with the music. I just played the music, made the song as good as I could, and stayed out of all the weird-ass business that was just nothing but horrifying to me. I didn't want to know what the managers thought. I didn't want to know about Courtney's goals and the difficulties between Eric and Courtney. We lost Patty during that time. It was just brutal. I tried to stay as far away from the business decisions and be present for the music.

I DON'T LIKE SAYING I'M ANTI-SOMETHING UNLESS I HAVE A SOLUtion. I'm hesitant to say I'm anti-capitalist because I can't think of a viable alternative, but I think it's safe to say that capitalism isn't working out for a lot of people. For most people. The corporate model certainly hasn't worked for musicians, and by its profit-driven nature, it remains unconducive to art and creativity. In the words of Shirley Manson, "The industry is a cesspit." Artists are forced into this arena in which gatekeepers allow or deny them access to broader audiences and the possibility of making a living. But every facet of rock culture, from record labels to media, by virtue of being a part of a global capitalist economy, exploits artists' labor for profit. If you make your record label a lot of money, you're golden. If you don't, you're expendable. This model is unsustainable, yet we all participate in it as creators, consumers, or voyeurs.

I imagine the commodification of alternative rock in pastoral, allegorical terms. The corporate model has evolved over time into a model of enclosure. The major-label systems were created well into the twentieth century, so they haven't been around that long, but by the 1990s, hundreds of record labels had been bought, sold, and consolidated into a handful. Now, in 2024, there are three major labels, and a lot of independent labels have distribution deals with these soul suckers.

Dig, if you will, this picture: A lush open pasture full of creative cows. These cows, they graze together, they explore corners of the pasture with friends and then maybe move to another corner and commune peacefully with other creative cows. One day, a farmer comes along and indiscriminately places a fence in the field. Now a fraction of the creative cows is stuck in a small area, maybe with other cows they've never met. Cows start sticking to certain corners of the pasture because it's dangerous to explore. Some other cow could steal what little grass you have. After weeks of grazing, creating, and eating, the little fenced-in pasture is filled with shit. There's no more grass, there's no more creativity, but the farmer is still getting paid, because the cows are still producing shitty milk and people outside of the fence are still buying it. They've grown accustomed to accepting shit that these trapped creative cows produce. They want more because they're starved for diversity, variety, beauty, and a reprieve from the late-capitalist hellscape in which they live.

Get it? The creative cows were the countless genres and underground scenes in the early '90s, and the farmer was a major-label representative who swooped in, contained, and categorized everything as "alternative rock women," which created an arbitrary and completely fabricated culture of competition. What might have happened if the cows had leveled the fence?

Chapter 5

ROCK FOR CHOICE

Untapped is the anger feminist power / A new
generation are screaming no / Dead men don't rape

—7 Year Bitch

I DIDN'T HAVE ANY CONCEPT OF THE STATE OF POLITICS AND THE battle for women's reproductive rights in 1991. I was ten. The B-52s' *Cosmic Thing* and Madonna's *Like a Prayer* were still on heavy rotation in our apartment, so I was aware of environmental issues and that dancing in lingerie with Black Jesus in front of burning crosses was scandalous (to say the least). My mom and dad married in the same living room I'd rock out to those albums in. I think my parents were Democrats at the time—I know they voted for Bill Clinton—and although they praise Ronald Reagan now, his eight-year presidency wasn't a talking point during my childhood. I certainly wasn't aware of the cultural backlash instigated by his "welfare reform," war on drugs, connection with the evangelical Moral Majority, and pro-life stance. I think they supported George Bush Sr. when he declared war in the Persian Gulf in 1990.

While I was busy playing soccer and dressing my guinea pig in doll clothes, a new wave of alt-rock women protested—and not for clicks, likes, or social media capital. Female-fronted bands in the 1990s were opinionated, vitriolic, and actively engaged in various political campaigns and social justice initiatives. Rock for Choice was a series of benefit concerts lasting from 1991 to 2001 featuring acts like Nirvana, Hole, Calamity Jane, Pearl Jam, Sheryl Crow, Alanis Morissette, Bikini Kill, Liz Phair, Joan Jett, 7 Year Bitch, Mudhoney, Salt-N-Pepa, X, Iggy Pop, Radiohead, and Kim Gordon and Free Kitten. Before she formed L7, Donita Sparks proposed a single show called Rock Against Coat Hangers. As a band, L7 decided on a subtler name and larger, continuing project. In 1993, Babes in Toyland, 7 Year Bitch, and Jack Off Jill produced a women-centered show where profits would be donated to a foundation of each band's choosing.

In 1992, Cathi Unsworth interviewed L7 for *Melody Maker* at a Seattle Fairground where they were performing with Sonic Youth and Mudhoney. Unsworth noted the dystopian-like conditions that plagued America during George Bush Sr.'s presidency, referring to the political and cultural climate as "something out of Jello Biafra's blackest nightmare." She referenced the televised beating of Rodney King by Los Angeles police officers, the subsequent uprising, and the repercussions Ice-T faced when he released his single "Cop Killer" (Bush Sr. personally condemned the song). This was the advent of parental-advisory stickers and Tipper Gore's campaign to protect America's children from profane music. She founded the idiotic Parents Music Resource Center in 1985, and in 1992, Washington state legislature passed a bill prohibiting the sale of "erotic" music to minors. Jennifer Finch called it "a very active part of political grandstanding. They can draw out an issue over here and make a really big deal of it, while, at the same time, they're passing through legislation."

In 1993, Dr. David Gunn was the first physician shot to death for providing abortion services. During 1992 and 1993, Rachelle Ranae "Shelley" Shannon was indicted in connection with ten counts of arson and acid attacks at nine abortion clinics in Oregon, California, Nevada, and Idaho. The surge in violent incidents against reproductive health clinics inspired members of L7 to initiate the Rock for Choice benefit concerts. After the overturning of *Roe v. Wade* in 2022, artists spoke out on Twitter and during live performances. Some, like Lizzo and Rage Against the Machine, donated half a million dollars to reproductive rights organizations. Others spoke out onstage, and the media defined those actions as taking a public stance against the ruling. What was lacking was a collective effort to support at-risk communities on the ground. Social media has created a more connected world but a more insular and individualized culture. It's easy to identify as a feminist, to share a hashtag or political stance in 280 characters on Twitter, but it takes work to organize. L7 never identified as women-fronted, feminist, or political, but their actions and activism over the course of a decade speak for themselves. While rock feminism now exists rather obsequiously in the performative realm of social media posts, it lacks the breadth, diversity, and nuance of '90s rock in which political activism was intelligent, inviting, and inherent in writing, production, and performance.

What was most unusual about the 1990s was how diverse rock music—and popular music in general—was. Despite attempts to retrospectively categorize the phenomenon as "grunge" and male dominated, women were active participants, and their catalogs contained multitudes. It remains a golden age in music and an era of artistic, creative control. The media had a difficult time corralling and categorizing the feminisms of '90s rock women in real time, and history has had a similar problem looking back. L7 played metal riffs and were dirty, androgynous, and absurd; Shirley Manson was direct, outspoken, and led Garbage, an all-male backing band that infused rock, pop, and industrial elements; Liz Phair was a hyperfeminine, overtly sexual singer-songwriter and sang about blow jobs and fucking and running; Courtney Love and Kat Bjelland first materialized as sludgy grindcore banshees, and they repurposed baby doll dresses and Mary Jane shoes, then emerging as twisted, snarling, Bette Davis characters catapulting the "kinderwhore" look into fashion magazines; the Breeders blended distorted guitars with vocal harmonies, and tinges of country, to redefine alternative indie rock; Throwing Muses started out in Rhode Island's hardcore scene as teenage outcasts playing twangy, creepy indie pop; in 1995, Kristin Hersh's original video for "Bright Yellow Gun" was banned on MTV because she smoked cigarettes and appeared to be in a relationship with a chimpanzee; two years later, nineteen-year-old Fiona Apple had a hit with her song "Criminal." In the video, she casually disrobes, takes photos of anonymous people in a wood-paneled room, and floats around in a bathhouse in a sea of disembodied men's legs. Even in an era of female success, sexual parameters existed.

Hole's "Miss World" video perhaps best captures the essence of women in rock in the 1990s by disrupting the literal pageantry of mainstream femininity: In the video, Courtney Love is the anti-pageant queen performing for a throng of moshing, stage-diving spectators. At the end, she is crowned and gifted a bouquet. It's *Carrie*—tragic yet celebratory—as Love sings the lines "I've made my bed, I'll die in it" in contrast with the glamour, she seems to recognize that all good things must come to an end. But the video exemplifies the legacy and cultural power of women in rock in the '90s. Watching it today is like unearthing a long-buried time capsule.

Alt-rock women didn't just make cool videos. They addressed issues pertinent to contemporary feminism. 7 Year Bitch formed in Seattle in 1990 and released two albums on C/Z Records before being signed to Atlantic in 1996. They were masterful social commentators, fusing blunt punk and metal riffs. The band released their first full-length album, *Sick 'Em*, in 1992, featuring the anti-rape classic "Dead Men Don't Rape":

> *You're getting sucked into society's sickest*
> *Don't go out alone you might get raped*
> *But not by a dead man 'cuz*
> *Dead men don't rape*

They got personal when they recorded and released their second album, *¡Viva Zapata!*, in 1994 in honor of their friend Mia Zapata (the Gits), who was raped and murdered while walking home in Seattle in 1993. Drummer Valerie Agnew also became one of the cofounders of the anti-violence and self-defense organization Home Alive, and the band played Rock Against Domestic Violence in Miami Beach with Babes in Toyland and Jack Off Jill.

L7's lyrics ran the gamut. Donita Sparks's "Wargasm" deals with, yup, war and American imperialism, comparing dropping bombs to sex, an absurdist commentary on the Persian Gulf War:

> Wargasm, Wargasm, one, two, three
> Smutty bloody pictures, ecstasy
> Blue balls waiting impatiently
> From Alcatraz to Lady Liberty
> Body bags and dropping bombs
> The Pentagon knows how to turn us on

Although the riot grrrl movements coined "Girls to the front," a phrase brilliantly appropriated by the Spice Girls in 1997, Jennifer Finch wrote "Everglade" about a woman taking matters into her own hands at a rock show:

> The guy was drunk, stupid
> And he must have weighed a ton
> Said, "Get outta here, girlie,
> I'm just trying to have some fun"
> So you wanna have some fun?
> Well, break out the big guns
> Rednecks on parade
> "Don't cross my line,"
> says Everglade

In "Seether," Veruca Salt's Nina Gordon unearthed her childhood alter ego, an inner rage that must be contained, and unleashed it in a pop masterpiece that simultaneously commented on prescribed gender roles and social expectations:

I try to keep her on a short leash
I try to calm her down
I try to ram her into the ground, yeah
Can't fight the seether
I can't see her till I'm foaming at the mouth

The 1990s heralded socially conscious storytellers aware of gendered embodiment. Kristin Hersh is as idolized for her cryptic lyrics as she is for her musical output; her writing is deeply personal, but abstract and poetic. Kim Deal—who, in my opinion, is the most underrated musician and lyricist of my generation—cut her teeth as the bassist and occasional vocalist of the Boston-based Pixies before forming the Breeders, a band that picked up where the Pixies left off. The Breeders music sounds simple, but it's a multilayered tapestry of acoustic and electric guitars and several-part harmonies. Deal's lyrics range from personal to social commentary, from earnest to absurd. I have no idea what "Iris," the first single off the band's debut album, *Pod*, is about, but I did name one of my bands Pod in the early 2000s. Deal has alluded to menstruation, to drinking mushroom tea and staying up all night, and it might also be a reference to the philosophical musings of Iris Murdoch. "Divine Hammer," a single from *Last Splash*, approaches themes of religion and existential dread—or maybe the search for a holy penis. Does it really matter?

I'm just looking for a faith
Waiting to be followed
It disappears this near
You're the rod, I'm water
I'm just looking for one divine hammer

Another thing that excited me about Kim Deal—and the entire Breeders band, really—was that they looked relatively normal compared to my kinderwhore idols. I'm what society refers to as a *late bloomer*. I lost my baby teeth late, I was about three feet tall until I was in high school, I didn't get my period until I was almost nineteen, and I certainly wasn't having sex, because I thought I would die being penetrated before achieving womanhood. I also wasn't very ostentatious. I had no sense of fashion—or sense of self, for that matter—and I couldn't imagine wearing baby doll dresses and bright makeup when I identified more with Kurt Cobain. The Breeders' style represented a different, understated feminism that spoke to me. They were three women in T-shirts and jeans, with a male drummer who looked like the captain of the football team, but what came out of their collective creative body was totally unique. I hadn't smoked enough cigarettes by 1993 to be able to scream, but the Breeders introduced another route into the rock club by way of bar chords and harmonies. That, I could do.

Kim Gordon and Liz Phair both have backgrounds in visual art. Gordon became the godmother of noise rock as bassist and vocalist of Sonic Youth, while Phair was crowned the queen of lo-fi indie rock in 1993. Gordon's music in Sonic Youth and her current solo work evoke the visual artist in her: alternative tunings, sonic and lyrical abstractions, with a keen awareness to gender and gendered politics. Sonic Youth released their major-label debut, *Goo*, on Geffen Records / DGC. By this point, Kim had transitioned from bass player to songwriter and contributed "Tunic (Song for Karen)" and the album's lead single, "Kool Thing." Gordon saw a sympathetic figure in Karen Carpenter, lead singer (and sister) in the '70s pop sensation the Carpenters. In the song, Carpenter plays the drums, makes famous friends in heaven, and reflects on her battle with anorexia. Gordon reflects on "Tunic" in her memoir *Girl in a Band*, "How was she not the quintessential woman in our culture, compulsively pleasing others in order to achieve some degree of perfection and power that's forever just around the corner, out of reach? It was easier for her to disappear, to free herself finally from that body, to find a perfection in dying." "Kool Thing" is kind of a diss track and a rolling commentary of capitalist patriarchy and misogyny. Apparently, Gordon met LL Cool J, a rapper she admired, and was so disappointed by his sexism and inattention to punk music (hip-hop and punk both emerged out of New York City in the late '70s) that she wrote a song about her disillusionment, even referencing several of his lyrics and albums. The bridge is an absurdist call and response between Gordon and Kool Thing (played by Chuck D of Public Enemy):

Gordon: Hey, Kool Thing, come here
Sit down beside me
There's something I got to ask you
I just want to know, what are you gonna do for me?
I mean, are you gonna liberate us girls
From male white corporate oppression?
Chuck D: Tell it like it is!
Gordon: Huh?
Chuck D: Yeah!
Gordon: Don't be shy
Chuck D: Word up!
Gordon: Fear of a female planet?
Chuck D: Fear of a female planet?
Fear, baby!
Gordon: I just want you to know that we can still be friends

Chuck D: Let everybody know
Gordon: Kool Kool Thing, Kool Kool Thing
When you're a star, I know that you'll fix everything

Chuck D's appearance in the three-and-a-half-minute video is poignant for a couple of reasons. First, in 1990, MTV and music videos were important. Collaborating with a member of Public Enemy was a throwback to the cross-pollination of punk and hip-hop that was prevalent in New York in the '70s and early '80s. Second, Sonic Youth are not known for short, radio-friendly songs, and it's likely that "Kool Thing" was chosen as the album's first single because of its length and special guest appearance. But anyway . . . Obviously, this song is political, but it's also tongue in cheek; this white woman is asking a Black man to liberate her from the confines that emerged out of a corporate, white supremacist state. Gordon takes her disillusionment, uses that, but also acknowledges the absurdity of mainstream white feminism. Clearly, I didn't get any of this when I was twelve.

I distinctly remember the first time I heard Liz Phair and the first time I listened to *Exile in Guyville* in its entirety. In 1994, I had a best friend named Anna. Anna had a cool older brother who listened to the Beastie Boys and Cypress Hill and smoked a lot of pot. Her older sister, Jane, was in college, and one weekend, Jane came home with Phair's second album, *Whip-Smart*. I had disavowed singer-songwriters by that point because alternative culture seemed to be all about bands, but "Supernova" intrigued me. This woman was singing about sex, but it was funny and explicit, and she played guitar. I eventually bought *Whip-Smart* and *Exile in Guyville* on CD and brought *Exile* with me on a family trip to Martha's Vineyard. It was there, in the third-row seat of a minivan, sitting next to my sister, that "6'1"" burst through my headphones. It wasn't love at first sight, but it was a shock to the system for sure. Liz Phair had a filthy fucking mouth, and like the Breeders, she looked like any other woman you might cross paths with on a college campus. What has always fascinated me about Phair is the discrepancy between her college-kid-turned-soccer-mom aesthetic and her unequivocal artistic, lyrical, and technical genius. This was obviously a completely bizarre twentysomething masquerading as a normal person. All along, she was taking notes, paying close attention to the culture, her music scene, and boyfriends.

This dichotomy presented yet another opportunity for me, as a thirteen-year-old fledgling musician, to participate in rock culture. You could embrace femininity and be taken seriously as an artist; be outspoken without screaming; you could play rock music without distortion; you could sing about blow jobs ("I want to be your blow job queen") and fucking and running ("Fuck and run / even when I was 17 / Fuck and run / even when I was 12") intelligently and with purpose. You could be a woman and tell stories—not everything needed to be autobiographical. Phair upended the archetypal femininity associated with singer-songwriters of the past and presented an entirely new blueprint emulated by contemporary artists like Soccer Mommy, Sadie Dupuis, and Mitski.

I did not think Alanis Morissette was cool in 1995. I'm not proud of this, but the "selling out" trope was rampant—even though the mainstream artists who promoted this idea were on major labels, but I wasn't a very discerning preteen. Morissette had been a television actor and pop star before transitioning to alternative rock with her third album, *Jagged Little Pill*, and while I listened to the album in private, in public I agreed with the middle school boys in Green Day cover bands who dismissed her as a corporate puppet. Thankfully, Morissette didn't need my opinion, and at twenty-one years old, she won Album of the Year at the Grammys. The album's most successful single was "Ironic," but the reason Morissette made such an impact was for the scathing breakup anthem, "You Oughta Know" that may or may not be about her relationship with Dave Coulier from *Full House* (gross):

> Did you forget about me, Mr. Duplicity?
> I hate to bug you in the middle of dinner
> But it was a slap in the face
> How quickly I was replaced
> And are you thinking of me when you fuck her?

Flea and Dave Navarro arranged the music, and Morissette's touring band consisted of the late, great drummer Taylor Hawkins. The video was filmed in the desert, the only shirtless band member was Hawkins, and you can barely make out Alanis's face beneath her long, black hair. Despite being young and angry, she avoided being sexualized, which, by today's standards, is almost entirely unheard of.

The grunge, alternative, and post-grunge influence extended beyond the borders of the United States. Australia had its own "women in rock" wave, and Brits like Elastica, Portishead, and PJ Harvey had success in Europe and the US. I heard PJ Harvey before I ever saw a photo, and I assumed it was a band. It certainly sounded like a band—drums, guitars, bass, and a female vocalist who didn't sound like anyone else on the radio—so imagine my shock when I discovered that Polly Jean Harvey was yet another singer-songwriter upending the singer-songwriter trope in her own unique way. PJ Harvey was almost painfully shy offstage, but onstage, she transformed into a five-foot-two conduit to some greater power that flowed through her and out of her mouth in wails, growls, and sometimes whispers. Unlike my other role models, she was outspoken about not being a feminist and not wanting to be aligned with feminism, because she rightly believed that doing so would pigeonhole her as a female artist or "woman in rock." However, her lyrics are explicitly feminist and deal with themes like body image, sex, female power, men, and masculinity. Judith Peraino wrote, "Her art and her very self appear thoroughly inscribed—'written all over' as [Mark] Paytress puts it—with body politics, and thus prepackaged by gender which obscures if not obliterates any other interpretations. Yet Harvey refuses access to that interpretation; she refuses to be 'drawn' by anyone but herself, and in this way, she perfectly fills the role of the unknowable Other."[1]

I have never wanted to write music criticism, and this is probably as close as I'll ever get to analyzing song lyrics. But if you look at a song like "Man-Size," it negates the whole "Is she or isn't she a feminist?" debate because the song speaks for itself: "I'll measure time / I'll measure height / I'll calculate / My birthright / Good Lord, I'm big / I'm heading on / Man-size / Got my leather boots on." Harvey is satirizing a macho, masculine identity and incorporating signifiers like dick measuring and big boots. In "50ft Queenie," the narrator demands that Casanova "bend over" so she can fuck him. "Rid of Me" is a contemporary take on the breakup song, but the narrator might be a socio/psychopath:

> Yeah, you're not rid of me
> I'll make you lick my injuries
> I'm gonna twist your head off, see
> Til you say don't you wish you never met her?

She performed the song solo on *The Tonight Show with Jay Leno*, and he looked a little freaked out. I loved it. In an oral history of Harvey's album *Rid of Me* with *SPIN*, she said, "When I was at art college, all I wanted to do was shock with my artwork. When I wrote 'Rid of Me,' I shocked myself. I thought, 'Well, if I'm shocked, other people might be shocked.' The sound of the words was powerful, and the rhythm felt clean and simple to roll off the tongue. I knew that this was the type of song I was trying to write."[2] With Harvey, the commentary on gender is right there, so she didn't really need to discuss it in the media.

FOR THE FIRST TIME SINCE THE HIPPIE COUNTERCULTURE OF THE 1960s, nonconformist, antiestablishment women got a mainstream platform, and they used that platform to participate in political and feminist agendas like Rock for Choice, anti-war demonstrations, and fundraisers aimed at raising money for domestic violence survivors. The musical diversity was also unprecedented. Because alt-rock women emerged from such diverse backgrounds geographically and socioeconomically, and because their influences were so broad, the music and lyrical stylings were capacious, pulling from punk, rock, and pop and emerging as unique forces in a cultural movement. Indie and alternative rock today is constrained by social media culture and an infatuation with the self and personal identity. Part of what made the '90s so unique is the breadth and diversity of the artists within the genre, but also the breadth, diversity, and nuance of its feminism as it emerged in the music and in performance. The mainstream visibility of these trailblazing women created an inclusive context for women and girls in the future to reference and emulate.

PART TWO

Chapter 6

WHEN IT WAS TIME FOR THE DOOR TO CLOSE, IT WAS SHUT

If ever a girlie wonder / Could ever be more
than just / One thing at a time.

—Tracy Bonham

IN 2003, THE (DIXIE) CHICKS SANG THE NATIONAL ANTHEM AT
the Super Bowl. Two months later, on March 10, ten days
before the Iraq War, Natalie Maines made a statement, criticizing then president George W. Bush during a performance in
London:

Just so you know, we're on the good side with y'all. We do not want this war, this violence, and we're ashamed that the president of the United States is from Texas.

The comments sparked a backlash that took the Chicks from the biggest concert draw in country music to relative obscurity in a matter of weeks. Despite numerous clarifications from Natalie Maines and the Chicks, pro-Bush, pro-war, pro-American groups and listeners called for a boycott of their music. Their single "Landslide" (a Fleetwood Mac cover) went from #10 on the Billboard charts to #44 in one week before disappearing from the charts entirely. Radio stations were bombarded with phone calls threatening boycotts if they continued playing the Chicks. Even radio DJs and programmers who sympathized with the band were forced to stop playing them, and some who continued giving the Chicks airtime were fired. In true democratic fashion, George W. Bush addressed the backlash in April 2003:

> The Dixie Chicks are free to speak their mind. They can say what they want to say . . . They shouldn't have their feelings hurt just because some people don't want to buy their records when they speak out. Freedom is a two-way street. I don't really care what the Dixie Chicks said. I want to do what I think is right for the American people, and if some singers or Hollywood stars feel like speaking out, that's fine. That's the great thing about America. It stands in stark contrast to Iraq.

The boycott led to the virtual demise of the band. They released *Taking the Long Way* in 2006 before going on hiatus. The album went gold in its first week, debuting at #1 on the Billboard country charts despite no radio play. In 2020, the Chicks released a new album, *Gaslighter*, and in June they changed their name, dropping the word *Dixie*, in an apparent distancing from an association with the Confederate-era South. The switch was made quietly, without an official announcement, with the release of a new song "March March."

The boycott of the Chicks is perhaps the most memorable incident of major fallout experienced by dissenting women in music following 9/11. But other music veterans spoke out against the war without consequence. Willie Nelson proposed an idea that 9/11 was a government conspiracy perpetrated by the Bush administration to drum up public support for a war in Iraq. Merle Haggard released an anti-war song in the summer of 2003 called "America First." Neil Young released an entire anti-war album, *Living with War*, in 2006, and Crosby, Stills, Nash & Young reunited for the North American Freedom of Speech Tour using the Iraq War as the backdrop. I attended that concert in Massachusetts with my sister, who complained the entire time, forgetting that CSNY have been anti-war since their inception. Any war, every war, forever. But I think we can all recognize the obvious gender differences between the Chicks and the rest of the dissenters. And I think it can safely be assumed that the Chicks' gender had a lot to do with the magnitude and longevity of their punishment.

Rock and roll is defined as rebellious, nonconformist, anti-establishment, and authentic. It can be mainstream and commercial, but its voice speaks from the social margins. However, it is a microcosm of larger society and culture—in all its sexist, patriarchal, racist glory and with all the inequitable trimmings. The Chicks, by definition, were rock and roll in that they vocally protested the Bush administration and the war in Iraq. Rock media acted as a mechanism for maintaining a climate of patriotism after September 11, and the repercussions the Chicks suffered because of their protest served as a lesson to those considering doing the same.

Retaliation against women's progress is an undeniable and recurring phenomenon in America. During the Revolutionary War eras, John Adams famously responded to Abigail Adams's plea to "Remember the Ladies" by vowing never to "repeal our masculine systems." After women found a sense of independence during World War II, when they were needed to fulfill men's jobs, they found themselves forced back into the home after the war—the intended audience of Cold War advertising campaigns encouraging them to cook and clean and respect their husbands and raise patriotic children. And look at what's become of the gains made by second-wave feminists: in June 2022, the Supreme Court overturned *Roe v. Wade*, which had been the law of the land since 1973, effectively taking away an individual's constitutional right to privacy and therefore abortion. I stopped watching *The Handmaid's Tale* during Trump's presidency. It seemed unhealthy to consume a fictionalized account of the subjugation of women in a totalitarian, fundamentalist state while living it—albeit without the bonnets and wool capes. Things were looking grim, and the likelihood of it changing seemed unlikely. There was a palpable attitudinal undercurrent bubbling up in mainstream media and into the streets. It was evident in Bernie Bros calling for Hillary Clinton's head. It was evident in the MAGA cult calling for the same. It was evident in the increasing visibility of Proud Boys, incels, white nationalists, and other not-so-fringe groups made up of "very fine people."

Things were supposed to get better once we all rallied behind a senile, eighty-year-old Democrat with a spotty track record (I still believe Anita Hill). But alas, here we are. At this juncture, both major political parties are beholden to corporations. One party is clear about their intentions to keep women at home, to force them to bear children, to frack the fuck out of the planet, and to openly deny civil rights to LGBTQ citizens. The other party pretends to care about social justice but uses fear to gain votes without ever *really* accomplishing anything because it's in their best interest to keep leftist bleeding hearts on their toes. Being a woman in the United States—and voting Democrat— is like being in an abusive relationship. Republican women have Stockholm syndrome—they love their captors and willfully participate in their own denigration—while Democrats remember the good times and hope they'll change. It used to be so great. Just one more chance. They promised this time. Next time. Soon.

Women live within the confines of patriarchy regardless of how much freedom or agency they have. There is a "patriarchal equilibrium" that waxes and wanes, affording women room, depending on the tide, to make their own choices.[1] The concept itself predicts powerful moments for women (and feminist men) but also an imminent rolling out of the tide. A feminist interpretation of the past suggests a "dynamically stable" pattern in the story of women's suppression: lots of small changes, moments of progress (like these little "women of rock" waves), but rarely a transformation in the status of women vis-à-vis men, as illustrated in the larger disappearing of women from the overall 1990s rock narrative, despite having been active participants on par with the boys.

The backlash experienced by women in rock consisted of various mechanisms from the aforementioned continuum to gender ideologies, assumptions about women doing "men's work," and the physical manifestation of government centralization, media consolidation, and the corporatization of the music industry in the mid-1990s. It was an abstract, multifaceted, ideological, attitudinal force that materialized in many ways. Backlash does not have to be overt, blatant, or violent—it does not always take the form of a clearly defined gender coup. A conspiracy against women does not mean that old white men in suits convene in underground bunkers devising how to condemn women most efficiently to the bowels of media in order to maintain the social order (although I would not be surprised if that were the case). Like racism, classism, and homophobia, misogyny and sexism have been built into the architecture of the country and its institutions.

RETALIATION AGAINST NONCONFORMIST, ALT-ROCK WOMEN BEGAN with the death of Kurt Cobain in April 1994. His wife, Courtney Love, and her band, Hole, released *Live Through This* that month as well. The death of the Patron Saint of Grunge and the success of his abrasive and controversial wife after his death led to an unfounded and completely outsized anti-Courtney campaign that continues today. Just as Cobain became the voice of a generation of feminist men, Courtney Love became symbolic of their downfall and the dangers associated with transgressive femininity. By 1997, Love shed her kinderwhore look in exchange for Hollywood glam after starring in Miloš Forman's major motion picture *The People vs. Larry Flynt*. She played Althea, Flynt's wife, achieved widespread critical acclaim, and was even nominated for a Golden Globe—she lost to Nicole Kidman. That same year, she appeared on the cover of *Rolling Stone*, alongside Tina Turner and Madonna, for a special "Women of Rock" issue, sporting her new, toned-down, Hollywood image. The band released their biggest commercial success, the

Grammy-nominated album *Celebrity Skin*, and toured the world in 1999. Hole's last *Rolling Stone* cover was published in February 1999. If you're Courtney Love, even if you comb your hair and wear Versace, you can't win in America.

Radio changed, too. While Bill Clinton subtly moved twenty-one-year-old intern Monica Lewinsky out of the White House and into the Pentagon to distance himself from temptation, he signed the Telecommunications Act into law in 1996. Within hours of the act's passage, the radio industry was overtaken by a feeding frenzy of acquisitions, as upstart corporations moved to buy as many stations as they could. While Clinton debated the meaning of *sexual relations* and the word *is* in front of a grand jury, college radio, which—before the ubiquity of household internet and social media—had been a primary source of promotion for underground bands, disappeared. Black- and women-centered stations were also victims of corporate consolidation. According to a lengthy report published in 2006 by the Future of Music Coalition, in 1995, Clear Channel owned 39 radio stations, more than any other corporation in America. Five years later, they owned 1,100.

In 1998, *Time* magazine published the story "Is Feminism Dead?" The cover photo featured the disembodied heads of Susan B. Anthony, Betty Friedan, Gloria Steinem, and Ally McBeal, a television character played by Calista Flockhart.[2] The article, written by a woman, Ginia Bellafante, generated a heated debate between the second and third waves and ultimately achieved what it set out to do: place the efforts of a decades-long, intersectional social movement on the shoulders of three white, cisgender figureheads and a fictional character, trivializing the expansive feminisms of the '90s and hammering the final nails into their coffins.

Woodstock '99 epitomized a violent shift from national feminism to national misogyny. The event took place over three days
in sweltering July heat, on an enclosed, retired military base. The
gender parity and diversity highlighted at Woodstock '94 had
been usurped by nu metal and frat-boy rape culture. The legacy
of the festival remains one of corporate greed, misogyny, sexual assault, and fires burning among rivers of shit. Oh, and only
three women performed, but who's counting?

Does mainstream representation matter? Well, yes and no. I
interviewed Cindy Wilson of the B-52s in 2018. In response to
my question regarding the band being unjustly ignored by the
Rock & Roll Hall of Fame, she assured me, "That's just corporate
crap." And at the time, I agreed. But for people without access to
higher education, the internet, or even the physical proximity to
countercultures and subcultures—or for those with only access
to mainstream media—representation and gender parity in
media matter a great deal, and for this reason, it is important.
Historically marginalized subjects—women, people of color,
queer, trans, and gender nonconforming artists—are further
marginalized by being siphoned off into supplemental categories, subjugating them as the "other" and keeping their access
to wider audiences out of reach. Representations of women in
media drastically shift during moments of war and political conflict. A few of these shifts occurred during World War II, the
Cold War, and the war on terror. While I recognize that gender
hierarchies existed before the 1940s, I'm using the "good war"
as an important turning point in which women's newfound
autonomy resulted in a backlash that pushed them back into the
home. This cycle of liberation and backlash occurred again in
the '80s after the rights and liberation movements of the '60s
and '70s, and again after the attacks on the World Trade Center

on September 11, 2001. These moments are predicated in a capitalist, patriarchal culture and its institutions, which continue to subordinate women at moments when masculinity is "threatened." The media is responsible for perpetuating myths, stereotypes, and misogyny that diminish women and maintain the status quo, especially when the nation is under attack. And since the country has been consistently at war or involved in foreign conflicts since World War II, it is unsurprising that women's representation remains virtually unchanged, although the methods used to prohibit their progress have become more covert and less recognizable. Unless, of course, you are a frustrated historian of gender with a keen eye for subtext. In the aftermath of the 9/11 terrorist attacks and the ensuing war on terror, the United States valiantly shifted to the earlier Cold War mythology of the protective male and dependent female.

The role of the media, whether it is explicitly aware or not, is to perpetuate encoded and internalized sexism. The public has been and continues to be indoctrinated with myths and veiled threats designed to push women back into their acceptable roles.[3] Historians searching the past for evidence about women have confronted again and again the unbelievable phenomenon of their apparent invisibility.[4] Feminist research has shown not that women were inactive or absent from events (social, political, or cultural) that made history but that they have been systematically left out of the official record. In the evaluation of what is important, of what matters to the present in the past, women rarely receive mention.[5]

Patriarchy is a cliché, but it is also a well-oiled instrument powering our cultural institutions. The dick machine grinds forward until the movement is briefly interrupted or brought to a halt by a pesky foreign object. Feminisms have periodically disrupted social order; disruptions perceived as threats to men and masculinity—and therefore national security—during times of war and conflict. The media is but one spoke in the proverbial wheel, diligently working to diminish women and uphold the status quo. Now more than ever, in the digital age of social media and a twenty-four-hour news cycle owned by a handful of corporations with direct ties to the politicians they serve, women's place remains tenuous indeed. Unfortunately, to date, backlash is the most reliable result of women's progress.

Chapter 7

GO ON, TAKE EVERYTHING

Burn the witch / just bring me back her head.

—Courtney Love Cobain

A S FAR BACK AS THE MIDDLE AGES, WITCH HUNTS—CONTRARY to popular belief—have had little to do with feudal superstition but are a phenomenon explained within the processes that laid the conditions of capitalist development.[1] Contexts in which women were accused of witchcraft include but are not limited to the expansion of private property; enclosure of land; war; and the first-, second-, and third-wave feminist movements. Witches were accused of sexual promiscuity, adultery, and of ambiguously influencing behavior: the behavior of white children, of white women, of religious men, of men in general, and so on and so forth. The accused were often unconventional, enslaved, single, nonreligious, or poor. In the twentieth century, the consequences faced by dissenting, feminist women shifted from being burned alive or drowned to being portrayed in media as power hungry, lesbians, and threats to men and masculinity, their reproductive capacities regulated by the state. Much better.[2]

As far as 1990s rock women are concerned, Courtney Love might be the wickedest witch of all and subject to one of the longest public witch trials in history. In an era when women were encouraged to work like men without losing their femininity, Love horrified audiences by brazenly pursuing fame and fortune, working her ass off, and paring hegemonically feminine ideals into their most disturbing elements: baby doll dresses, torn stockings, barrettes, ruffles, and severe makeup. Courtney Love was able to bring all this into mass consciousness because it happened to be marketable during a moment when alternative music was considered a viable commodity. In response to her success, she has been accused of many things: (1) influencing young girls to be loud, drug-taking feminists; (2) theft—specifically of stealing the songs and souls of every rock star guy she ever fucked; (3) murdering her husband; and (4) castrating a generation of men, a sentiment shared by mainstream media after 9/11.[3] The media and the general public subordinate her to men—her husband, male colleagues, the industry in general—and the end result is perhaps the most damaging of all: a personality that overshadows her work in Hole, one of the most important bands of the decade.

Meanwhile, Billy Corgan's relentless egocentricity has resulted in some funny memes, but that's about it. Eddie Vedder can bring a barf bucket onstage every night, puke, and keep singing, and no one cares (I do care, and I hope he's okay). Kurt Cobain's legacy is not overshadowed by his self-loathing, heroin addiction, and suicide (I love Nirvana, too; I'm just making a point). People don't even hate Nickelback as much as they hate Courtney Love, and Nickelback is the most hated band on the planet. I'm not defending Courtney Love as a person. I don't even know her. I'm just desperate for people—especially the people who despise her—to acknowledge the glaring double standard. I don't like Hillary Clinton, nor do I support her policies, but that doesn't blind me to the fact that she has experienced sexism and misogyny in the political sphere. It was hard to miss during the 2016 presidential debates.

In order to break down the contempt against Love, it's important to know where she came from. She is a mythical character. As I mentioned before, I read Poppy Z. Brite's *Courtney Love: The Real Story* when it was published in 1997, and her childhood was so dysfunctional that it's almost funny. She grew up in a hippie commune. Her biological father was a freeloading, drug-dealing, occasional Grateful Dead band manager who gave Courtney acid when she was four. Her mother, Linda, came from a wealthy family—later, Courtney's grandparents provided her with a trust fund of $500 a month, which is how she traveled to Europe. Her parents divorced when she was eight, and her mother moved to New Zealand, leaving her behind. Troubled-teen Courtney was shuttled around from boarding school to boarding school, to juvenile delinquent centers and back again, finally ending up at an institution for wayward girls. In the early 1980s, she traveled to Ireland with her friend Robin Barbur, at the invitation of Julian Cope of the Teardrop Explodes, and experienced the postpunk Liverpool scene. Love once said: "Before Liverpool, my life doesn't count. Ian McCulloch and Julian Cope taught me a great deal. I owe them a lot. Liverpool had been a great school to become a rock star."[4] In 1982, she caught a bus to Heathrow, stopping off for egg and chips in the English midlands. At the airport, she wrote in her diary: "I can play music and understand technology. I can stay in and resist the temptation to make the first move or stay too long or worse get intense. I can make tea now. I can remain enigmatic, pose well, and appear feminine." She thinks about all the people she met and concludes: "There's one asset everyone has until they've spent it. Their mystique."[5]

She made her way to Los Angeles and was cast as Nancy Spungen's best friend in *Sid and Nancy*. In 1987, she played the role of Velma in Alex Cox's *Straight to Hell*, costarring alongside Joe Strummer and Dennis Hopper. Courtney met Jennifer Finch (who would later join L7) and Kate Bjelland (Babes in Toyland) in the early 1980s. They started their first band, Sugar Baby Doll, around 1985. By the way, if you weren't unapologetically stealing the whole candy, doll, lace, and lipstick thing that Love and Bjelland had going on, were you even a fifteen-year-old girl starting a band in the early '90s? Sugar Baby Doll didn't last, and Bjelland moved back to Minneapolis to start her band. Love may or may not have joined Babes in Toyland and been fired, but either way, she moved back to Los Angeles and put an ad in the *Recycler* ("I want to start a band. My influences are Big Black, Stooges, Sonic Youth and Fleetwood Mac") and stripped to pay the rent. The original incarnation of Hole (Jill Emery, Caroline Rue, Eric Erlandson, and Courtney) was extreme and less melodic than the *Live Through This*–era Hole. The band released *Pretty on the Inside* on Caroline Records, an independent label and subsidiary of Virgin. Courtney's singing is a mix of shouting, screeching, and rasping. The band's musicianship is apparent, and her lyrics read like twisted poems. The late, great Elizabeth Wurtzel reviewed the album for the *New Yorker*, writing "*Pretty on the*

Inside is such a cacophony—full of such grating, abrasive, and unpleasant sludges of noise—that very few people are likely to get through it once, let alone give it the repeated listening it needs for you to discover that it's probably the most compelling album to have been released in 1991."[6] Love entered the music scene abrasively and completely antithetically to the submissive, heteronormatively sexualized women of mainstream pop culture.

Of course, Hole was lumped with Babes in Toyland, L7, the Nymphs, and other female-led underground groups. Although these bands were quite different from one another and wildly competitive, they were all dubbed "foxcore" by Thurston Moore. The name caught on, and it is something I hope he regrets to this day. Hole played around LA, but they weren't discovered until they went to England in late 1991, where Love was perceived as a true original.

By late '91, she was dating Kurt Cobain and had established a reputation for shocking audiences. She didn't attempt to pacify the general public or patriarchal notions of feminine propriety— she twisted gender norms, punched people, aggressively pursued fame (and men), thrust her leg on a monitor, and screamed. Love upturned the agreed-upon notion of how popular female icons should behave, and she's been punished for it, as her personal life continues to take precedence over Hole's cultural impact.

Hole ignited the first-ever bidding war over an unsigned female band. In the music business, independent labels are not considered contenders—until you're on a major label, you're considered "unsigned." Madonna's new company, Maverick, was the first to be interested in signing Courtney Love to a major record deal. Clive Davis, president of Arista Records, reportedly offered a million dollars to sign the band. Rick Rubin, head of

Def American, was interested, but he and Courtney didn't get along. She had similar difficulties with Jeff Ayeroff at Virgin, who called her a bitch. It's unclear whether or not most of the bidders liked, or even knew, Hole's music—it was the magic combination of Madonna's interest, her affiliation with Kurt Cobain, and the strength of Courtney's personality.

Hole signed a million-dollar record deal with DGC; she married Kurt Cobain and, within the realm of the alternative music scene, was regarded as a crazy, soul-sucking bitch. In September 1992, Lynn Hirschberg published "Strange Love: The Story of Kurt Cobain and Courtney Love" in *Vanity Fair* in which Love admitted to using heroin during the first few weeks of her pregnancy. In the photo session, the very pregnant singer posed in a negligee and bra, holding a cigarette in her left hand. The fallout from Hirschberg's article was devastating. Love and Cobain temporarily lost custody of their daughter.

April 8, 1994. I remember the day Kurt Cobain's body was found. I was thirteen and a blossoming fan of Nirvana, but as a nerdy, flat-chested wannabe musician, I was more interested in Courtney Love and her almost all-female band, Hole. Still, Cobain's death affected me in a couple of ways. First, it felt as though the air had been sucked out of the world. His music, his feminism, his creativity, and his moral fortitude brought out the best in everyone, but it certainly brought out the best in men. Even the douchebag boys in my school became more feminist. Their musical tastes expanded, they thought women were cool, and they disavowed misogyny. The second emotion I felt was fear. I'm a historian, but I'm also in recovery, and I find myself spouting off sayings like "Feelings aren't fact." But they can be.

Fear and anxiety can be a physiological reaction to perceived harm.

I felt uneasy when Kurt Cobain died, and I felt uneasy about Courtney Love's vilification, but I didn't have the knowledge or the words to articulate it (*misogyny*) at the time. Love had been skewered in the press long before her husband's suicide. Kurt and Courtney were both heroin addicts, but Love's transgressive femininity, drug addiction, and outspokenness positioned her as an unfit mother and a succubus, draining the lifeblood from the Patron Saint of Grunge. She has been called a murderer for thirty years—if there were any actual evidence to suggest she had anything to do with her husband's death, I guarantee she would be rotting away in a jail cell. That's how much a lot of people hate Courtney Love.

By the time the band's second album, *Live Through This*, was released in 1994, Love was a household name. Unfortunately for her, her husband died by suicide the same month her album was set to be released. The subject matter—I mean, even the album title—seemed to presuppose her predicament. She did live through it, the album was a multiplatinum success, and Hole's follow-up, *Celebrity Skin* (1998), was nominated for four Grammy Awards, a sign of having truly conquered the mainstream. By 1996, Love had cleaned up her image, taken on Hollywood, and earned a Golden Globe nomination for her role in *The People vs. Larry Flynt*. In 1997 she wore a classy white Versace gown to the Oscars and became the face of the brand. What all this adds up to is a pretty fucking successful career.

Women—especially unlikable women—who succeed in a big way disconcert convention. When women succeed as Courtney Love did, we eagerly await their downfall. We don't say it out loud, but we want them to die. We did it to Amy Winehouse. We

turned her into a Halloween costume. An internet clock antici-
pated her demise, and then she did die and became a martyr. We
martyr our women out of guilt and because we fear their greatness. Women who defy social norms are threatening. We fear
them. Even when public meltdowns or existential tumult doesn't
result in death, the media still tends to regard them as duplici-
tous at best. These women must have done something—fucked
someone, killed someone, married someone—to get where
they are.

Perhaps Courtney Love's greatest sin is that she didn't die.
Because her artistic contribution to the rock genre throughout
the 1990s is important. Not only in my personal opinion, but
actually objectively important. Maybe more important than
Nirvana, because we expect male genius. Her treatment by the
public is emblematic of the treatment of many high-profile pioneering women in music; instead of attacking them on the merits
of their music, they are made into frivolous caricatures. It's hard
to critique the greatness of *Pretty on the Inside* and *Live Through
This*; it is easy, however, to focus on Love's behavior in a way
that undermines her credibility as an artist. The condemnation
of Love—a '90s rock figurehead who recorded one of the seminal rock albums of all time—after her husband's death, accelerated a broader anti-feminist sentiment that led to more tangible
economic, social, and political consequences for other alt-rock
women of the '90s.

Chapter 8

PIMPS AND HOS

Monica Lewinsky is a fuckin' ho and
Bill Clinton is a goddamn pimp!

—Kid Rock, Woodstock '99

WHEN I WAS AROUND SIX, I STARTED FAKE SMOKING MY AUNT'S cigarette butts. This was back when ashtrays were considered décor, so old butts were always within reach. I thought it was very mature to stand around smoking, and it remains my longest, unhealthiest on-again, off-again relationship. When I was twelve, we all lived in the Boston area, and Aunt Wendy started dating a bass player named Gary. My mom brought me into the city to see one of his shows, and I was infatuated with this group of old men (in hindsight, they were probably in their early thirties), playing indie rock at a tiny club in front of twenty people. Three years later, Aunt Wendy went to Woodstock '94 with friends. I think she brought me back a T-shirt. She said it was muddy but didn't have any other major complaints. The concert was held on a farm, most of the attendees were able to scale a fence and enjoy the music for free, and only three people died! What a success. The Woodstock series has never boasted egalitarian lineups—there were only nine women onstage at the original concert in '69—but Woodstock '94 did include diverse artists and some major female players like Sheryl Crow, the Cranberries, Deee-Lite, and Salt-N-Pepa. A lot of female audience members took their tops off, but male audience members didn't see it as an invitation to grope them.

Michael Lang, an original founder of Woodstock '69 turned corporate whore, and lifelong corporate whore John Scher made a vow to repeat the show in five years, but the musical landscape had changed significantly. Woodstock '99 was meant to celebrate the thirtieth anniversary of the original Woodstock festival and was touted as a joyous occasion that would replicate the "peace, love, and happiness" of 1969. Woodstock '99 was doomed from the start. The event took place over three days in sweltering July heat, on a retired military base, which provided ideal infrastructure—an enclosed installation surrounded by a fence that had been painted and named "the Peace Wall"—ensuring that all attendees paid the $130 ticket fee. Cost of attendance, $4 bottles of water, "Show us your tits" chants, and the intense heat exacerbated a general sense of anger and discontent. Only three women appeared at Woodstock '99—Jewel, Sheryl Crow, and Alanis Morissette—with one woman performing per day, as if to fulfill a quota. The headlining acts were Limp Bizkit, Korn, Metallica, Megadeath, and Kid Rock. James Brown opened the show—and in what world does James Brown open for any of these people? Despite his laughable, curated Muppet-meets-rapper affect, Fred Durst successfully started a riot during Limp

Bizkit's performance of "Break Stuff," in which he encouraged the crowd of 225,000 mostly white men in backward baseball hats to "take all that negative energy and let that shit out of your fucking system." Attendees began tearing the place apart, literally, and crowd-surfed on large pieces of plywood, grabbing any breast in sight along the way.

The legacy of the festival remains one of disaster, corporate greed, middle-class white misogyny, sexual assault, bonfires, looting, rioting, and rivers of human excrement. The three days of mayhem resulted in 3 deaths, 1,200 admissions to on-site medical facilities, 44 arrests, numerous accounts of sexual assault, and 4 reported rapes. It was covered in real time by *SPIN* magazine journalists David Moodie, Maureen Callahan, and Mark Schone in an article I revisit often. Recent documentaries, *Woodstock 99: Peace, Love, and Rage* and *Trainwreck: Woodstock '99*, present revisionist narratives, in hindsight. The films star predominantly male narrators and attendees. Jewel and Maureen Callahan make appearances, but both read like apologist tales of accountability and atonement by well-intentioned men (performers and attendees alike) who participated in the violence but have since matured—very much "Boys will be boys" and "Sorry I lit those fires and grabbed those titties." Sheryl Crow and Alanis Morissette are missing, as well as in-depth interviews with female attendees. In her Women of Rock Oral History Project interview, Luscious Jackson drummer Kate Schellenbach recounts the sea change that took place in 1999 and her Lilith Fair tour mate's assessment of Woodstock:

Kate Schellenbach: There were all these stations in the mid-'90s, this whole subgenre of stations that were playing women alternative rock. Everything from Hole to Garbage to all the female singer-songwriters. That all went away pretty quickly by the time that fucking Woodstock '99 thing happened. We had done Lilith Fair, and that was incredible. One of the people that was on Lilith Fair the second year was Sheryl Crow. She played Woodstock in '99, reported back, and was just like, "This was horrible. Women were literally getting groped and fucked in the mud pits. It was just awful." We all had a sense that "this is not good."

ONE MONTH AFTER WOODSTOCK, ADAM HOROVITZ, OF THE ALL-male group the Beastie Boys, accepted the MTV video music award for best hip-hop video, and at the urging of his longtime partner Kathleen Hanna of Bikini Kill, addressed the assaults from the stage: "I read in the news and heard from my friends all about the sexual assaults and rapes that went down at Woodstock '99. And that made me feel really sad and angry. OK? Are you all there? OK." While the '90s brought a feminist wave and thoughtful, progressive male rock stars to the mainstream, Woodstock '99 removed the mask from a generation of young men who had supposedly been listening.

Tracy Bonham: I think maybe even the bigger situation would be that the radio changed. Everything now was like angry white boys with baseball caps backwards, Limp Bizkit. I think there was a backlash, and I'm not saying this because I'm bitter. It's just that there was this whole, you know, "women in rock" thing, and I was constantly fielding these questions: "What does it feel like to be a woman in rock? Lilith Fair? Yeah! Girls' club." And then when it was time for the door to close, it was, like, shut. And then it was like there's only one of you that might make it through the cracks. Maybe that's Alanis Morissette. She can have a longer-lasting career, but everyone else, no. Now we're just going to play Limp Bizkit and Korn. I called it *Cookie Monster rock*. It was a dark time for me. I went to a Radiohead concert once at Hammerstein Ballroom, and I was bawling because it was so good. It was so musical and soulful and what was playing on the radio in the States, and what was so popular, was so angry. I was crying for music.

In 1997, the culture at my suburban high school shifted. I was studiously making music with my band, Thriftshop Apocalypse, and avoiding homework. We played one show in our brief career, under a gazebo with two all-male bands—one was a ska band, the other metal. The metal guys were the nice, supportive ones. While my musical taste had been acceptable a year or two earlier, it became a source of shame. Boys didn't like Veruca Salt, Hole, or even L7. The radio was overtaken by Marilyn Manson, and mall goth usurped kinderwhore and grunge fashion. In '97, my bass player told me she was going to see this new band Limp Bizkit with friends. Lindsey had/has great taste, so I bought *Three Dollar Bill, Y'all* at the mall, went home, popped it in my Fisher CD / double cassette deck, and was horrified. The big hit was a cover of George Michael's "Faith," and I loved George Michael. My grandmother had a full-length poster of him inside her closet door. I didn't appreciate how these rapping, rocking straight men had bastardized my precious gay pop dad. The rest of it was even worse. Needless to say, I didn't go to the Worcester Palladium with Lindsey, but my reasoning consisted of two distinct parts: (1) I didn't like the music; and (2) I had a feeling I would get hurt at this kind of show. As much as I wanted to get out of the house for the night, my fear of bodily injury won. Korn was another popular band among the formerly artsy music nerds at Hanover High. I didn't understand this either, and I wouldn't have felt safe at a Korn show, a band fronted by another seemingly sex-obsessed guy ("A.D.I.D.A.S." was the first Korn song I ever heard) who freaked the fuck out onstage and, purposefully or not, gave license to an army of high school boys to express their misogyny openly.

The Woodstock '99 music festival has gone down in history as "the day the '90s died" the same way Altamont came to mark the end of the free-loving '60s. I think a lot of the criticism of Woodstock '99 looks for material excuses: bad planning, Limp Bizkit, the unrelenting heat, and a poor understanding of the zeitgeist, which created a bubbling cauldron of violence. And I suppose some of the political and cultural context did present a backdrop upon which the violence emerged: the Monica Lewinsky scandal and Bill Clinton's subsequent impeachment—the fact that a twenty-two-year-old intern was effectively blamed for the decisions of a man who could have been her father and happened to be the president of the United States; the success of the *Girls Gone Wild* franchise; the paranoia surrounding Y2K (nothing happened); the apparent period of prosperity for middle-class Americans (I've always been poor, so the low unemployment rate and overall economic prosperity wasn't something I experienced personally while I was washing people's shit-stained underwear and slinging porn at a video store); and the Columbine massacre, the first major school shooting in the country, occurred three months before the festival. A nonprofit group handed out candles to the crowd to commemorate victims of gun violence on Sunday night. Instead, many attendees burned whatever they could find, and huge fires broke out. Red Hot Chili Peppers encouraged the crowd of 350,000 by playing their sped-up version of Jimi Hendrix's "Fire."

What gets lost in examinations that focus on cost, weather, the economy, the bands, and the violence is the spiritual, psychic, endemic impetus behind the violence itself, especially the violence against women. Many Women of Rock Oral History Project narrators, even those who weren't in attendance at Woodstock, noted an energetic shift in '99. Subjects interviewed for the Woodstock '99 documentaries commented on the "feeling" in the air. A palpable tension and rage. I felt it in my last year of high school.

We moved to this tiny little house on an inlet in Rhode Island my senior year. I was still very attached to my alternative/grunge heroes, and I proudly wore these influences on my sleeve—and plastered them all over my car. It took about two weeks for me to gain a reputation as the "new girl" / "dyke" at Mount Hope High, and senior boys were not shy about sharing their feelings with me in the hallway between classes. When boys liked Nirvana, they never insulted me to my face, and that was fine with me. What I didn't do, as a young woman, was react with violence. I didn't shoot everyone in my high school, I didn't grab guys' dicks at shows, and I've always been averse to making messes in public, because there are people working minimum-wage jobs who have to clean up after us.

Let me preface what I'm about to say by announcing that I fucking hate Limp Bizkit, in case that isn't clear. But I don't think the violence at Woodstock '99 is the fault of Fred Durst. I don't think Fred Durst, alone, is powerful or intelligent enough to incite that level of chauvinism. I don't think the violence is Red Hot Chili Peppers' fault, or Korn's fault, or even Kid Rock's fault. The misogyny and the rage seemed to materialize without provocation and for no reason other than "the physical discomfort of entitled, frustrated white men who had never been inconvenienced in any remarkable way before."[1] What Woodstock did was put all those dudes in an enclosed (there's that enclosure theme again) area where they could anonymously destroy their surroundings and rape women against a soundtrack that encouraged that behavior. But this shit happens all the time at concerts and festivals. It's the anonymity—whether behind a computer screen or invisible in a crowd—that gives the entitled license to be cruel. But it's the entitlement itself that's the root of the problem. White men feel entitled to certain things—certain inalienable rights, if you will—and expect their God-given position at the tippy-top of the social pyramid (any pyramid, really). White, middle-class men feel helpless, unappreciated, disregarded, and threatened when women achieve any type of progress. And women in rock in the 1990s made that progress—they even surpassed men, creatively—and inspired a generation of people to embrace feminism, to denounce sexism, racism, and homophobia. The violence against women at Woodstock '99 could have been a consequence of the collective frustrations of the festival's attendees; it could have been the aggressive music, the overflowing portable toilets and lack of water, but misogyny is endemic. The underlying thread tying the assaults, destruction, and bonfires together is an ideological sense of divine entitlement created by white men and passed down from generation to generation. The country is founded on it, its institutions and economic systems are built around this understanding, and its survival depends on strict, impermeable gender hierarchies. Sometimes these hierarchies are enforced using rape. So yeah, to echo Kate Schellenbach, in '99, I had a feeling something was happening, and it wasn't good.

Chapter 9

WE ALREADY HAVE OUR LADY GROUP

All the radio stations were like, "Well, we're already playing Garbage, so we can't play Luscious Jackson." It was that kind of thing. "We already have our lady group," or, "We're playing No Doubt, so we can't play you."

—Kate Schellenbach

Tanya Donelly released *Star*, Belly's first album, in 1993, on Sire/Reprise. The album sold five hundred thousand copies and was nominated for a Grammy in 1994. While half a million is a lot for an indie band, it was not a massively successful album by major-label standards at the time, but the Grammy certainly should have garnered the band respect in the industry. Donelly arrived at my apartment in western Massachusetts on a humid summer day in 2017 because—and this is a great example of how kind she is—she didn't want me to sit in Boston traffic. The "grunge" renaissance had officially arrived, and Belly reunited to record their first album in twenty-one years. So the interview was celebratory in many ways, but we also discussed the nagging disease (sexism) that the industry never seems to be able to shed; in fact, it does a pretty good job of massaging it into its very architecture. Much to my surprise, Donelly had nice things to say about her management and representatives at Warner Bros. and Sire but was critical of the major-label system itself, including reductive marketing tactics that painted women in rock in broad strokes.

Tanya Donelly: I am not a fan of the model. The major-label model was broken. But the people that we worked with at Reprise and Sire and Warner Bros. were some of the smartest, most competent people that I've ever worked with. It was different than for 4AD also, so I can say all those same nice things about 4AD, but it was definitely more of a family. Warner Bros. had a more clearly corporate structure, but they just very wisely assigned to us the people that clicked with us. We became very close to the PR department, Deb Bernardini, who lives up here now. She comanages Wilco, and she's doing a festival this weekend. She's one of the most—just the highest level of integrity and love of music and competent, sane. The people that were assigned to us, for whatever reason, just knew what they were doing and were in it for all the right reasons. And the higher up you get, the less that is the case.

I sat in meetings back then where people would say to me and my manager, "Well, we have too many women on the radio right now. We're going to hold this song back because there are too many women right now." And then listing, "So-and-So's got a single, So-and-So, dah, dah, dah, dah, dah, dah." I was so stunned by the interaction itself. Just that someone would say those words to me. It was ridiculous. And I'm going to guess that it's possibly not radically different now. It got to the point where I was just like, "I'm not going to talk to those people anymore. I'm going to deal on the level I'm comfortable with and let our manager take these meetings."

THE SCARCITY MYTH—THAT THERE'S ONLY ENOUGH ROOM FOR ONE or two women at a time—creates a culture of competition among women, which is then perpetuated in the media. In a capitalist economy, an economy dependent on sexual divisions of labor, mainstream rock media exists to serve the interests of the ruling class: rich white men. The scarcity myth is a tool designed to devalue women's contribution in what is still considered a male-dominated industry. We're all aware of the "mean girls" trope: women are jealous and tear one another down. They don't support one another. They gossip, scheme, and catfight. Men don't have to fight with one another because there's room for all of them, all the time.

I saw Liz Phair at a club in Boston in 2018. She brought Juliana Hatfield onstage to perform a duet, and they both acknowledged the fact that, in the '90s, they competed because of the scarcity myth. Meanwhile, there were nine thousand male-fronted bands trying to sound like Eddie Vedder. Unfortunately for us, there was room for all that hot garbage. I seriously doubt that Stone Temple Pilots or Bush (the second wave of alternative men) sat in a meeting with their management and were told that their singles were being held back because there were too many men on the radio at the time. By the late '90s, women were told this repeatedly.

Women suffer more when markets are consolidated or privatized, and women in rock certainly felt the effects of record-label consolidation in the mid-1990s. The global music business constitutes a powerful oligopoly—a market condition in which a few firms dominate most of an industry's production and distribution. Major record labels make up over 85 percent of the music industry. In the 1990s, the four major record labels (known as the Big Four) were EMI, Sony Music Entertainment, Universal Music Group, and Warner Music Group. Universal Music purchased EMI in 2012, leaving the Big Three: Sony BMG, Universal Music Group, and Warner Music Group. Major labels oversee subsidiary labels—there are many of them—giving consumers and music fans the illusion of choice. It's like walking into a grocery store. What's on the shelves may give the perception of endless options and brands, but really, a handful of companies control a vast majority of sales.

When "poor performance" closed a subsidiary, its artists would be distributed among the other subsidiaries under the major label. In this respect, the hierarchical structure of a major label can be quite complex and draped in secrecy, with bands being moved from label to label without their knowledge or consent. At the end of the 1990s, women in rock found themselves in this predicament.

Tracy Bonham: There was a changing of the guards like three or four times, and then they sold it [Island, Polygram, and associated labels were purchased by Seagram's, and under the Universal Music Group umbrella], and then it merged with Def Jam. So now there's like hip-hop people in the same offices as the rock people. And they were trying to figure out who they were as a label.

Kate Schellenbach: Capitol Records had gone through person-nel change, and the people who had championed us throughout the years left or were fired. They were left with us and didn't quite know how to market us. They basically were like, "We're going to stop working this record." All the radio stations were like, "Well, we're already playing Garbage, so we can't play Lus-cious Jackson." It was that kind of thing. "We already have our lady group," or, "We're playing No Doubt, so we can't play you."

PHAIR RECORDED HER LAST "HYBRID" ALBUM, WHITECHOCO-*latespaceegg*, in 1998. By 2003, she found herself alone on Capitol Records. She experienced another bout of backlash after releas-ing a corporate pop album, *Liz Phair*, but the decision to deviate from her indie roots was less an artistic decision and more of an economic imperative. She was figuring out how to navigate a changing industry.

Liz Phair: I didn't sign to Capitol. I signed to Matador. And then during *Whip-Smart*, Matador signed to Atlantic, because back then, all the major labels were buying up indie labels. So it was very normal for these suddenly successful independent labels to be affiliated under the umbrella of a larger major label. Atlantic was my first hybrid major label with Matador. But that had noth-ing to do with me. That was just Matador doing their business, getting their money, getting greater distribution. There were two camps in indie rock—and this is why I keep getting in trouble—there are the camps that see it as alternative business, right? And they accept the marketplace. They're just in a different niche part of it. And then there are people that reject the marketplace entirely. And they are in indie rock because they reject the marketplace. And I write music made by both. But I was more of the, like, "accept the marketplace" thing.

When Matador left Atlantic, I was still on Matador, and I went with them. And then they were looking for a different home. And in fact, Capitol Records was the one that I was like, "Anything but that." And that's the one they picked. And they gave me a hefty bonus for it because they knew that I was one of the valuable artists that they wanted, and I was not happy about that. But the trouble came. So *Whitechocolatespaceegg* was like another hybrid working situation, which Matador had already been. I was used to that. And every label was doing that. And then what happened was that didn't go so well, and it was clunky and difficult to move two rivers in the same direction. So you had the Matador indie river, and you had the major label, Capitol, river. And they did not seem to go in the same direction easily. And there I was, straddling the two. Like, "Okay, guys, that's pretty wide." And then Capitol and Matador separated. But I was part of the deal to separate. And I was alone then on Capitol Records. I did not do this. Suddenly, Matador was like, "All right, we're parting company, but, Liz, you're going to stay with Capitol because they feel like they've invested in you for the last record." So now I'm on a major label by myself. And right at the 2000s period when indie's over, in a way. Of course, not the people that were anti-capitalist to begin with, which is why I'm always getting in trouble. I was in the other camp, which was a legitimate place to be in, where a lot of them were. That was definitely what was bifurcating that alternative rock community. But anyway, I was trying to get as much creative freedom while still being more amenable. Like, "Okay, so now we're doing pop. Okay. I like pop, too." I didn't have the kind of issue, the territorial issues that many people in the music business have. It was like their sports team; they would ride and die by their scene.

And because my upbringing had been very different from this, I didn't know professional artists. I knew art appreciators. And to me, as long as the emotional truth was in the song—I just do not understand how you can look at mainstream art like the Beatles, create arbitrary lines between this being great art and this being commercial art. I don't know where those lines are, because it seems to me that every type of artist makes great and bad art. I just don't get it. And if they make something that's not great, you don't have to hate them.

Shirley Manson: We got sold by Almo Sounds to Interscope, which was a massive major label. Jerry Moss, who ran Almo Sounds, did not ask our permission. He didn't say, "I'm thinking of selling my label," or give us any due warning. He sold us to Interscope Records, and there was absolutely nothing we could do about it. So having been this massive band on a small label, we became a small band on a massive label that was in the business of pop commercial success.

The music industry is a cesspit pretty much. I mean, if you just think about what it is, for a label to compete, they need to want to be the biggest and they want to be the best. And if your label isn't wanting to be the biggest and the best, you're probably not at the right label. So it's a commercial enterprise, and it preys on the desires of musicians to have their work heard. And it's a nasty relationship, much like a pimp and a streetwalker, and it's pretty simple. And you have to decide as an artist, well, am I willing to get into bed with a nasty old pimp for a couple of years to see if I can reach an audience? And then I'll worry about the consequences later. Which I think is what most artists do. And then unfortunately, the powers that be, and commerce and so on and competition, they are powerful forces, and they can often corrupt the artist, or they'll destroy the artist. And so therefore, it's kind of a nasty business.

Major labels affected thriving independent labels by making it impossible for them to compete with astronomical advance offers to bands that were, often, unable to make a living. Consequently, some indie labels made a deal with the devil, so to speak, in exchange for financial backing. When Nirvana began to achieve success in the late 1980s, they were signed to independent label Sub Pop. Their 1989 album, *Bleach*, sold well enough for the band to move to a bigger label. Signing with DGC Records (an imprint of Geffen), Nirvana released *Nevermind* in 1991 and found itself thrust into the mainstream. In less than a year, the album had sold more than four million copies (compared to thirty thousand copies of *Bleach*), knocked Michael Jackson's *Dangerous* from the top of the Billboard chart, and the rest is history.

For Sub Pop, Nirvana's success was a blessing and a curse. The label had begun layoffs in the spring of 1991, reducing its staff to a core group of five employees. With the royalties it received from *Nevermind*, along with the buyout from Nirvana's contract, and potential royalties from any future albums, Sub Pop was pulled back from the brink of collapse. However, the carefully crafted niche that Sub Pop had found in the music industry vanished as major labels, eager to discover the next big thing in grunge, offered unsigned bands large advances that smaller, independent labels couldn't compete with. Sub Pop chief Bruce Pavitt said of one band, "I was told by our head

A&R agent that they would be happy with a $5,000 advance. Two months later, we were giving them a check for $150,000."[1] In 1995, the company sold 49 percent of its shares to Warner Bros. in exchange for financial backing.

Radio consolidation also affected alt-rock women, specifically. The Telecommunications Act enabled Clear Channel—now the iHeartRadio / Live Nation conglomerate—to become a behemoth. Seldom in the annals of American history has a piece of legislation with such wide-reaching consequences passed with such little public notice, in no small part because the media companies that might have reported on it critically had an interest in not doing so. Newspapers and television (not to mention the phone companies) were affected dramatically in ways that allowed the largest corporations to grow even larger. But none were affected as much as radio, where the ownership caps that had prevented any one company from achieving a dominant position were removed altogether.[2] Before the proliferation of household internet in the early 1990s and social media, college radio had been the primary source of promotion for underground bands. By and large, it disappeared. Black- and women-centered stations were also victims of corporate consolidation. According to a lengthy report published in 2006 by the Future of Music Coalition, in 1995, Clear Channel's enormous size was enough to make people who care about media diversity nervous. But it was the ways in which they cut costs and boosted profits, and their conservative political leanings, that gained them a reputation for corporate villainy.

While women's issues are not the focus of Naomi Klein's *The Shock Doctrine*, the relevance of her theory to women's lives is clear. Women suffer more when economies are privatized and governments reduced.[3] A recent example comes out of the post-9/11

US, "when U.S. President George Bush used the terrorist attacks to build a labyrinth of private security companies that have made huge amounts of money while stripping citizens of their civil rights."[4] After 9/11, rock radio served to uphold new national interests—state-sanctioned surveillance, patriotism, nationalism, and anti-feminism. Censorship and restrictions on artistic expression are most effective when they are imposed within a highly concentrated marketplace directed by the federal government, and the corporate consolidation of radio reached its peak after September 11, 2001, with Clear Channel owning and operating radio stations and businesses in over sixty countries.[5] The owners of Clear Channel had a bond with the Bush administration and the Carlyle Group, a global private equity firm with George Bush Sr. on its payroll.[6] This led to an alliance of conservative agendas and censorship illustrated in the "164 songs that were banned from American Radio after 9/11."[7] The rise of Clear Channel coincided with the "cultural troika" of media, entertainment, and advertising, declaring the post-9/11 age an era of neo-'50s nuclear family, domesticated femininity, and Cold War warrior manhood.[8] Although male musicians were also victims of censorship, women suffered the additional backlash against third-wave feminism after 9/11 and ensuing, albeit ambiguous, war on terror.

SOME THINK NAPSTER AND DIGITAL DOWNLOADS KILLED THE record industry, but here's a controversial take on the advent of music streaming: Napster didn't kill the record industry; the record industry killed itself. Napster came at the end of a decade of expansion and profits in the global music industry. The CD had become an enormously popular format; almost one billion were sold in the US in 2000, and at around sixteen dollars an album, they weren't cheap. The '90s gave birth to many classic albums, but not every LP was deep-pile quality from start to finish. People were paying a premium price for a CD that might contain only two or three songs they wanted (I cannot personally relate to these kinds of people). The lure of free music proved enticing to fans, and the music industry was slow to respond to the looming crisis. As former *Rolling Stone* journalist Steve Knopper wrote in his book *Appetite for Self-Destruction: The Spectacular Crash of the Record Industry in the Digital Age*, the way the music industry dealt with Napster paved the way for a series of disastrous decisions the industry made as the sheer scale of the digital threat started to become clear. Here's what they could have done: paid their artists more money and made CDs more affordable while investing in digital alternatives. Instead, they sued Napster, and then they started suing regular-ass people.

Though A&M Records filed the first lawsuit against Napster, it was a band's campaign that captured the public's attention. Individuals were sued by record companies as well—teenagers, moms—resulting in multimillion-dollar lawsuits still in litigation today. Metallica took Napster to court after finding an alternative mix to their song "I Disappear" on the service—a version that had never been officially released. On April 13, 2000, Metallica filed a lawsuit against Napster for copyright infringement, racketeering, and unlawful use of digital audio interface devices at a district court in Northern California. Metallica then tracked down the names of 335,000 Napster users who had shared their music and asked Napster to ban them from the service (which Napster did). Metallica's crusade created a backlash, with some of their own fans seeing it as a personal attack against them. Record companies (and Metallica) could have been "smarter about dealing with Napster—if not licensing content to it directly, then doing a better job of creating a competing, cost-effective service rather than just stonewalling and treating the Internet as a threat."[9] They dealt with file sharing almost exclusively through lawsuits and copyright protection. None of this worked—I mean, it was like Daddy Warbucks taking a bunch of little orphan Annies to court—and record executives spent years losing serious business to Napster before Steve Jobs came along in his black turtleneck with the iTunes Store. Although Napster didn't survive, its legacy lives on in Apple/iTunes, Spotify, YouTube, and social media, which dominate how we discover music today. The music industry finally figured out how to profit from this new platform. In conclusion, artists get paid even less now than they did in the '90s, and their livelihoods depend on touring and selling merchandise to make a living.

The reason that all this shit happened in the first place is the removal of regulations that limited the monopolization of industries by corporations. The fundamental condition for the existence of corporate monopolization is a functioning, capitalist economy. And the fundamental condition for existence and development of capitalist society is its ability to undermine and destroy the condition of reproduction and uphold white, male corporate supremacy. This took me a long time to wrap my head around, but it's important to look at women in rock as a subservient class of laborers in a male-dominated industry. For the capitalist institution—the music industry, record labels, and their counterparts, radio and print media—to profit while upholding the status quo, they must devise tactics to discontinue women's ability to reproduce themselves as valuable contributors to the rock genre. By treating women as novelty acts, trivializing their work, sexualizing them, exploiting their labor, and documenting their careers in terms of archaic

notions around womanhood and femininity, their contributions become subsumed, secondary to the mainstream historical memory of rock. This means that success, longevity, and
relevance are guaranteed to a small portion of the population:
white men. Reproduction of the workforce—in this case, mainstream rock musicians, and yes, they are workers—and the
entirety of rock culture mirrors capitalist patriarchy and its
dependence on a clearly defined working class, sexual and gendered divisions of labor to uphold ambiguous national values,
and long-held gender ideologies.[10] If mainstream rock culture
did the things that it purports to do—rebel, dissent—women
would be the figureheads and symbols against which male rock
stars are judged. Women are inherently antiestablishment pre-
cisely due to their gender, and they buck against the system by
recuperating rock ethos, rearing electric guitars or drumsticks
(sometimes with children in tow!), subverting expectation.
This can be marketable, which is great for business, but not so
great for maintaining the ever-tenuous sexual hierarchies that
the state depends on to keep women in line.

Chapter 10

"I'M A SLAVE FOR YOU": WOMEN IN ROCK POST-9/11

After September 11, they stopped playing nonconformist women on the radio. I mean, that's just a blanket rule of thumb . . . And so that sort of put a full stop to all the alt-girls of the '90s. That was the end of the run, and it's open to argument whether we've even recovered from that yet.

—Shirley Manson, Garbage

MELISSA AUF DER MAUR LEFT HOLE IN THE SUMMER OF '99, AT the height of the band's career. That year was also the height of Courtney Love's career as a movie star, and Melissa found herself not playing and performing music as much as she'd like, living on a $600-per-week salary while contractually obligated not to record or write any music outside of Hole. Pretty fucking boring if you're a musician. Coincidentally, D'arcy had just left Smashing Pumpkins, and Billy Corgan needed a bass player for their *Machina / The Machines of God* tour. Auf der Maur jumped at the chance to make some real money and challenge herself creatively, and she embarked on the rigorous yearlong tour.

She quit music after her stint with the Pumpkins, citing her unhealthy relationship with it—being thrust into the corporate music industry at a young age—and returned to photography. Her first opening was in Brooklyn, New York, on September 10, 2001, and the following day, she watched the Twin Towers burn from the roof of the Chelsea Hotel. The tragedy incited a new appreciation for the opportunities she had been given as a musician, and she started poring over old demos for a solo album. Her first record, *Auf der Maur*, was self-financed (she made more money than she ever had before with Smashing Pumpkins) and eventually released on Capitol Records in February 2004.

In July of that year, Auf der Maur joined the Curiosa Festival tour, curated by Robert Smith and featuring the Cure, the Rapture, Interpol, Mogwai, Muse, Thursday, Cursive, Cooper Temple Clause, and Head Automatica. But by 2004, alternative music was "officially not happening."

Melissa Auf der Maur: I don't know if it was the digital era or the corporate blowout after all those big signings in the '90s. I mean obviously there was the White Stripes and the Strokes, but that was very vintage and nostalgic, but alternative music was not on the airwaves. I was the only woman on this tour in 2004. It was a remarkable eight-week tour across the US, and not one music journalist other than *NME* came to document it.

The Cure were headlining, and there was no press; the venues were half-empty. Nobody knew what was happening, because it was before the internet. It was like the internet had happened, but alternative people were still alternative, so they didn't have access, and nobody—not *SPIN*, not *Rolling Stone*—covered it. Robert Smith lost so much money doing it, and he just wanted to bring the Lollapalooza era of rock music to the US and the people. Although the venues were only half-filled, the audiences were really happy. It was like, "The alternative people are still alive, they're here," but they barely knew it was happening. And it happened to be the greatest tour of my whole career.

GARBAGE RELEASED THEIR SELF-TITLED DEBUT RECORD IN 1995, during the crest of the mighty "women in rock" wave, and it sold four million copies worldwide. *Version 2.0*, their second full-length, sold just as well. By 1998, Shirley Manson was a celebrity. At the top of their game, the band decided to take some risks with *Beautiful Garbage*, the follow-up to *Version 2.0*—it's a huge risk for a major band to be creative and not simply repurpose their previous album—and (surprisingly) received positive feedback from their record labels and managers. But the cultural shift happening in music, with its anti-woman underpinnings, would be expedited by the attacks on the World Trade Center.

Shirley Manson: When we finished the record, our record labels came and heard the record. Our managers came and everybody was like, "Whoa! This is incredible! It's incredible!" We sent advance copies to journalists. We got amazing reviews. And then we were set to launch the record on September 13. And we woke up on September 11, 2001, like the rest of the world, and the world had completely changed. Amongst much more important things (i.e., changing the world and devastating people's lives), one could say the same thing about what it did to our career at the time, because it just killed the momentum of that record release. And we never really regained that release opportunity again. By the time the world had sort of reconvened, normal service had resumed, we had missed our window of promotion and opportunity, and that record, although it sold a million copies, was seen as a massive commercial failure. Record labels get really greedy. And they're like, "Well, yeah, you sold thirty-five thousand records last week. But hey, No Doubt sold fifty-five thousand."

The conservative political climate that arose after 9/11 killed us as a pop band for sure. After September 11, they stopped playing nonconformist women on the radio. I mean, that's just a blanket rule of thumb. They stopped playing anyone who disagreed with the mainstream. We were unable to get on the radio. And so that sort of put a full stop to all the alt-girls of the '90s. That was the end of the run, and it's open to argument whether we've even recovered from that yet.

I'm not entirely sad that happened, to be honest. But at the time, it was devastating, because you just feel like, "I'm never going to recover from this. My whole career is now over." By this point, I was in my midthirties, and I'm like, "I'm screwed. As a woman, I'm screwed." Women don't get to come back from thirty-five and a completely disastrous career. It just doesn't happen in the music business. And I convinced myself of this. As it turns out, it was completely wrong. But you don't know this at the time, and it's difficult. It's difficult to sustain the blow of a public fall from grace. It's embarrassing. It's uncomfortable. Your identity is locked up in how people perceive your band. It was a very, very tough time in my life for sure.

L7 RECORDED THEIR 1997 ALBUM, *THE BEAUTY PROCESS*, AS A TRIO following the departure of bassist Jennifer Finch. They toured with Marilyn Manson and released *The Beauty Process* documentary in 1998. Although the album received rave reviews, it didn't sell, and they were dropped from Reprise Records. They released their sixth album, *Slap-Happy*, on independent label Bong Load Records in collaboration with Wax Tadpole. In 1999, nu metal was on the rise, and women in rock were descending into an abyss left behind by a dramatic cultural shift.

Donita Sparks: The dissolution of L7, we just—there was no money, there was no support. We were dropped from our label. We fired our manager. It was just, you know, the wheels-fell-off kind of thing. We had no savings. We had nothing. I knew I'd never do a reunion, so I thought, *Eh, we'll put it on hiatus.*

Liz Phair: Post-2001, post-9/11, I would say if there was a culture that I noticed, it might have been patriotism. I don't know that I would go just male-female, because I feel like the '90s were about male-female. Maybe the era post-9/11 was a sort of patriarchal patriotism. But what was really driving it was America coming to terms with an outrage and coming to terms with what we've done with our foreign policies, how 9/11 was inevitable. And with the information age, there was a return to that bedroom pop that started it in the first place, because recording studios in the 2000s became ubiquitous. Suddenly, it felt to me like the bar to professional music production had just gotten super low again in a way that I find really appealing, and in a way, that produces a lot of great work. A million voices suddenly were heard that weren't heard before. So in a way, even though it went back to a backlash, I saw another hopeful spring of the home recording studio flourishing and a lot of voices being elevated. It hurt me financially. I didn't like that. That sucked for me. But for the industry, I feel like we have a ton of voices we wouldn't have had without that shift.

IN 1991, "SMELLS LIKE TEEN SPIRIT" IGNITED A GLOBAL, CULTURAL shift and changed the mainstream music landscape. The song was a call to arms, and the video featured the band in a dimly lit school gymnasium, surrounded by moshing fans and anarchist cheerleaders. Nine years later, the Backstreet Boys graced the cover of *Rolling Stone*, suited up but with their pants around their ankles, under the headline, "The New Teen Spirit." Boy bands, female pop stars, nu metal figureheads like Slipknot, Korn, and Staind, and some members of the old guard—namely, Aerosmith and U2—graced the covers of *Rolling Stone* through the early 2000s, but nonconformist women disappeared. It was like the feminist, alternative rock wave never happened. The only lasting relic was a commemorative issue honoring the ten-year anniversary of *Nevermind* and an exclusive interview with Krist Novoselic and Dave Grohl. It's true that sometimes pop usurps rock and vice versa, but in the past, there had been room for multiple genres in the mainstream. I remember watching the MTV Video Music Awards religiously from like 1987 to 1995, and the nominees ran the gamut. Even after the grunge explosion, Madonna, Janet Jackson, New Kids on the Block, Salt-N-Pepa, Sinéad O'Connor, Metallica, R.E.M., Guns N' Roses, and

Michael Jackson (the list goes on) remained highly visible super-stars. There was room for everyone. This leads me to posit that the complete disappearance of alternative rock women from the mainstream was more dictatorial than the simple effect of an organically changing culture. Because the cultural shift was drastic, violent (see Woodstock '99), and overtly misogynistic.

In 2002, Christina Aguilera appeared on the cover of *Rolling Stone*, lying on red silk sheets, nude except for a thick studded bracelet and a guitar, under the headline "Inside the Dirty Mind of a Pop Princess." I don't think Christina Aguilera plays guitar, and if she did, I don't imagine she'd play it naked. There are no other women mentioned on the cover, but Bowie, Eminem, Nirvana, Tom Petty, the Hives, Bright Eyes, and the Foo Fighters are listed under the word "Plus" in bubble letters. The same year, Shakira, Britney Spears, Mary J. Blige, Avril Lavigne, Ashanti, and Alanis Morissette appeared in the special "Women of Rock" issue. Morissette was arguably the last surviving relic of the "angry women in rock" phenomenon. In perhaps the most blatant manifestation of Cold War gender roles in mainstream media after 9/11, singer, entrepreneur, and reality-television star Jessica Simpson appeared on a 2003 cover in her underwear, Swiffering, under the headline "Housewife of the Year."

Throughout American history, in the wake of war or global conflict, marginalized people are blamed for the collapse of American values thought to keep the country safe. Japanese Americans were interned during World War II; gay people were subject to scrutiny and fired from their government jobs during the Lavender Scare; in the 1980s, Black women were branded "welfare queens"; and women remain consistent targets of the conservative ideologies of Republican motherhood / cult of domesticity. During times of national panic, women are urged to return to their "natural" place, at home, barefoot, and pregnant—definitely not with electric guitars. Because non-conformist women, as a group, reached the formerly unreachable heights of mainstream visibility in the 1990s, they had to be intentionally submerged beneath the banality of patriotic country music, nostalgic indie rock, and harmless pop. New forms of femininity—the sexy, barely legal kind—were promoted. Old, stereotypical rock gods regained their rightful places on magazine covers, and boy bands reintroduced the male gaze, six-packs, and air humping.

Post-9/11 radio played insipid male indie rock, sad-boy emo, and the remaining rock women who survived the backlash and carved out space for themselves in the post-9/11 landscape. Sheryl Crow transitioned fully to adult contemporary and even released a country-inspired duet with the biggest asshole on the planet, Kid Rock, in 2001; Liz Phair went corporate pop punk with her 2003 album *Liz Phair*. She wanted to earn more money for her work (the gall!) and hired the Matrix, a songwriting team best known at the time for producing songs for Britney Spears and Avril Lavigne, made a boatload of money, and of course suffered the consequences. Avril Lavigne's skater boi punk was molded out of the most palatable relics of alternative music; Gwen Stefani released her first massively successful solo album (*Love. Angel. Music. Baby.*) in 2004. I was working in the Newbury Comics warehouse at the time, and everyone loved that record. By the mid-2000s, hypermasculine misogynist rock receded and gave way to a wave of predominantly male, vintage-inspired indie rock. Bands like the Strokes, the Hives, and the White Stripes performed lo-fi nostalgia on MTV and *Saturday Night Live*, while singer-songwriters like Elliot Smith (who is great) and Ryan Adams (who sucks) found commercial success via film and television commercials. Nu metal became a bit more thoughtful and sensitive, and now there's a whole generation of grown adults who genuinely like Staind, Linkin Park, and My Chemical Romance. The field of rock music was once again male dominated, only this time, it was apolitical, and inarguably vapid and capitalistic.

In the year 2000, I moved to Providence, Rhode Island. I lived in a small room with holes in the walls, peeling floral wallpaper, and a window that wouldn't open, for $150 a month. I groomed dogs by day, played in bands by night, and spent all my money on whiskey and cigarettes. By the early aughts, I was exclusively listening to vinyl and had learned to keep my real influences a secret. It was a privilege to be one of the few girls in the scene who was a musician and not a girlfriend. Unfortunately, I thought it was important to maintain my place in the boys' club, and it really had become a boys' club once again. I enjoyed the scene in Providence at the time, but still, there was a feeling that something was off; something wasn't right. I couldn't go to a noise/ grind show without getting pummeled or seeing a dick onstage; nor could I stand in the front row without getting tea bagged, so I stood on the sidelines. I think I saw more penises between the years 2001 and 2003 than I've seen in my entire life.

I remember going to a friend's house on a Saturday night in 2001. They were having a party to celebrate this new band, the Strokes, performing on *Saturday Night Live*. The band wore leather jackets and an air of indifference. I expected something loud, or at least unique, but what came out was a perfectly enjoyable pop song called, "Is This It," which is exactly how I felt by the end of the performance. My guy friends were impressed. Later, I found out the Strokes were all rich—not that it really matters, but it explains the number of opportunities they received.

Life is probably easier when your dad is John Casablancas. The White Stripes were more up my alley, and I vaguely recall seeing them live in the early 2000s at Lupo's Heartbreak Hotel. I was belligerently drunk and very impressed.

Shortly after, everyone in Providence started dressing like Spock from *Star Trek*, doing cocaine, and listening to A Flock of Seagulls. Ever late to the party, I didn't start doing cocaine until 2006. The legacy of the post-mod fad means there are a lot of people my age who don't have any eyebrows, but most of the bands that came out of the genre haven't lasted. The White Stripes were the first of the lo-fi nostalgia wave—and Jack White has proven himself to be an innovator and genius—but bands like the Hives, the Vines, Franz Ferdinand, and Interpol kind of rode the crest of the wave and then receded back into the underground. Nothing in the mainstream was moving, feminist, or political. There was this return to '80s decadence disguised as outsider art that was actually quite commercial. The only artists I remember being excited about were Peaches, Outkast, Missy Elliott, this female-fronted hardcore band called the Red Scare, Mary Timony's solo albums, and the Breeders, who have consistently released records without major-label support.[1] I gave up on radio, MTV hadn't played music videos in years, and I gave up on the culture I loved while simultaneously embarking on a pretty dark downward spiral that landed me in detox in 2007. Needless to say, the early 2000s are a little blurry.

Kate Schellenbach: We weren't as big as Hole or somebody who could do a tour and make money and do a stint in Vegas or something. We were never big enough to be able to do that. When the band split up, I think initially I was sort of lost. I didn't quite know what to do. I didn't think I wanted to be in a band, because it was such hard work and all the touring. I wasn't up for it. A band people say is like a marriage, but you're married to several people. I always like to equate it to working in an office, but then you never leave the office, and the office gets on wheels and travels to the next city. I was enjoying not doing that. I was playing drums for people and recording and just sitting in with people and just trying to keep my chops up as a musician. It took a few years to find a different career. I was living in New York. I started dating someone in LA, so I started coming out to LA more and more. Then I eventually moved out here. Through a variety of different people and things, I started working at *The Ellen DeGeneres Show* as a researcher. Then I started a second career as a whatever, third career, as a TV producer, talk show producer. That's what I've done for the last fifteen years. But it took a few years to be like, "Who am I? What am I?" I mean, I think I feel really lucky all the things I learned on the road and being in a band that produced themselves and put on shows. I was very much involved in all of the day-to-day scheduling and touring schedules and all this kind of thing that gave me a producer's brain.

Donita Sparks: We had a manager taking 20 percent off the top of everything, pre-expenses. We had—everybody gets a cut before the band does. We never sold a million records; I think *Bricks Are Heavy* sold 350,000 records. That does not set you up; that doesn't do shit. A little money has come in because we've been on some video games, and "Shitlist" was in *Natural Born Killers*. Just a little bit, but not enough to support the band, or anything like that. So no, we didn't. Then there are bands like White Zombie who sell a few million records and they're set up for life, and yet, is our name as big as White Zombie? [*makes* *scale tipping gesture*] Is our name bigger than White Zombie? Is White Zombie—I'm friends with those guys, but is their name mentioned in articles these days? They made money. We didn't make money. Because we didn't sell records. But I don't say we didn't sell records; I say our record company didn't sell records, because we busted our ass, we worked really hard, and we toured a lot and wrote good songs. I never understood why we didn't get bigger, because I was like, "Well, shit, we've got catchy songs. What's the problem?" So I don't know if mainstream media were ready for us. I don't know if they're still ready for us. Sometimes I think we were too threatening. But that could be just crazy talk. We didn't wear makeup, or we wore fright makeup. How is media going to deal with that, you know? Where does that fit?

So the wheels fell off. We were forty and had no health insurance. We had no savings. We had nothing. So what do you do? You have to reassess your life at that point. And I called it a *hiatus* because I always said I would never do a reunion.

Tanya Donelly: The demise of Belly was a combination of things. I abandoned the helm, and by the end of it, there were factions not speaking and hadn't spoken to each other for an entire tour. That's all behind us now. Luckily, we've all moved well beyond it. Belly started with such passion and love, and we were just crazy about each other and had so much fun, and then I think we panicked about how we were going to sustain it. I think that's how it feels to me now. We felt this obligation to sustain this level and keep things moving forward.

What we should have done is sequester ourselves and just be like, "Okay, we're going to write a bunch of songs together, and no one else is going to have anything to do with that." We did to a certain extent. But then the second album, *King*, was very much like, "How are we going to keep this going?" And when it didn't keep going, I think we just also started to feel there was some crack in the foundation that we kind of made up.

There were cracks, but nothing that we couldn't have mended if we had had the energy. I mean, again, we had an eighteen-month tour. There was a lot of anger, and we just couldn't figure out a way to approach each other about that. People make fun of Metallica for having a mediator come on tour with them. Honestly, I'm like, "In the right hands, that could have been everything." My husband always says, like, "Bands need doulas, someone to come in and just facilitate."

Tracy Bonham: I started recording in 1998 for the second record, but because of everything happening at Island Records with the selling of the company and the merging and all of the consolidating, it was shelved. I mean, they finally released it. But during those two years, from 1998 to 2000, I was basically told to go hide my head under the sand and wait for it all to clear and to see what was going to happen by the dust settling with the merger and, "Oh, things are changing in the radio." And this is where my manager, who I told you about, I should have fired him right then and there, 'cause he's the one that said go hide and wait it out.

And he said, "You're only as big as your last hit." And I wish I hadn't listened to him, because I honestly think if I would've just kept playing, even if it was smaller venues, just kept the momentum going and stayed connected with my fans, my career would have been completely different. I lost all those people. A lot of those original fans were kind of radio people. So they're not super committed to, like, the artist, but I lost them. So finally, my album was allowed to come out in 2000. At this point, everything had changed. It was Island Def Jam. They didn't know what the hell to do with me. Nobody wanted to really hear from a strong woman. And then the rest, it was like, I mean, they basically like pulled all funding after the first single, and they were like, "We're going to drop you." So I did go on tour with that album. But I just remember being pretty miserable. It came from having this huge success with, like, people saying yes to me and "Yes, your video can be on this and that. And you can play here" to "No, your video can't even be played on MTV." And those kinds of things hurt because I had these expectations and hopes, and it just was like a slap in the face. And it took me a while to recover from that stuff.

Zia McCabe: *Thirteen Tales from Urban Bohemia* did quite well. Courtney did quite well on the publishing side of things. And he wanted to own a space, rather than rent a building, and put a studio in it. I was picturing like an old gas station or something, because the spaces we'd been in weren't that big. And when I walked in here, I was like, "Holy cow, this is a quarter of a city block." We built the Odditorium in 2000/2001, out of what was an old machine shop. We started using our video budgets to do all the interiors rather than make throwaway sets. It became everything. There's a studio, there's a green screen, so we can do videos. Where the wine bar is now used to be a bank of offices. We had our management in house and an assistant in house. There's a room in the back where the merchandise shipped out of. We have the industrial kitchen and dining room so that we could have, you know, David Bowie over for dinner, which we have done, and the Strokes. So many cool bands have come here and played music and feasted. And of course, we can rehearse and make our albums. So it became our clubhouse that we can do everything. Every aspect of being in a band, we can do out of this building. And that was the dream. And we're still living it!

Shirley Manson: There's a patriarchal system that has been put in place that allows men to thrive. And women historically have been kind of eradicated from the narrative in all areas of life. Whether it's science, whether it's math, whether it's arts, whether it's history, our voices have been drowned out. And therefore, it continues to be very difficult for women's legacies to be even acknowledged, let alone stick around.

I think we reared our children to believe that the highest currency for a woman is beauty and youth. And when she loses her beauty and loses her youth, we are encouraged to believe we are then, therefore, we have no agency and it's all over, and we're on the rubbish heap, and we are of no value to culture and society. And I feel like women themselves have bought into this. I think they've allowed themselves to believe that this is the case: "Oh, when I have a line on my face, I'm no longer of interest to anybody." And I think deep, deep down, we really believe that.

And I think, therefore, women don't always stick around to compete when their bloom of youth starts to fall away; they literally go and hide. And they stop trying, and they stop competing, and they allow themselves to be shrunk by a sort of patriarchal system of control. And I mean, I'm talking in very dramatic terms, and I think there's also very subtle things at play, but I do think essentially that's what has gone on. So if you're not sticking around long enough, it's hard to be seen as this amazing artist who's made their mark on music or fashion, or like I said, science and so on and so forth. If you've disappeared to have children or you've just stopped trying, then female competition gets eradicated, and it's the male totem pole that stands and is worshipped.

To be fair, Garbage never broke up ever. We just had a very frank conversation. Which was, we were on tour, it was really unpleasant, we weren't getting along well. And I said to my band, "I'm going home. I've had enough, I'm going home. This is not fun. And I don't want to make another record, because I feel like if we make another record and put it out, it doesn't even matter if it's *Sgt. Pepper's Lonely Hearts Club Band*, it's going to be rejected. We are out of sync with the culture. We need to go home, re-educate ourselves, invest in life, relearn the rules and think again." And that's what happened. We just went home, and because we weren't getting along, we didn't even contact one another.

And then the years passed, and my mother got dangerously ill, and we knew she wasn't going to last much longer. She had a very aggressive form of dementia. And so I didn't even think about making music; I was just sort of trying to get through life. And then when my mom died, a whole spate of other horrendous things happens to those we loved. One of our friends lost their six-year-old kid, my best friend from home lost her young husband. It was just one thing after another. We were always at funerals. I mean, it was mad. And, of course, when you're in pain, you want to be creative. And I really started to miss the band and miss the fun. And finally, I went to Coachella, and I watched a whole day of Coachella, and I was looking at the bands and thinking, *Why have I allowed the music industry to make me think that I'm not as good as whatever is going on here? Because I know I am. And I rarely feel confident, but I can smoke 99.9 percent of anyone here today.* And it just made me think, *You know what? Fuck this. I'm going to go and make music. And I don't care if I'm not successful. I don't care if people think I'm a loser. I need to do this.*

And I was at a memorial for my friend's six-year-old son, who lost his life to Wilms' tumor. And I had been asked to sing a Bowie song—"Life on Mars?"—to honor Pablo, their son. And I sang at the memorial, and it was intense. Butch was there, and I bumped into him, and we sort of looked at one another, and he was like, "I want to be making music. And it was so good to hear you sing." And I was like, "Yeah, I want to be making music, too. Why are we not making music? This is mad." And he went, "You call Steve, I'll call Duke." And I was like, "Okay."

And then that was basically it. We just got back together again and started working. And we had a very sort of punk rock attitude, which was, "Fuck everybody. I don't care if they say we're shit. Let's just do something that makes us feel good." And that's what we focused on. And then we've just sort of rebuilt our career on our own terms. We're completely independent of everybody and anything. We're free, we run free, and that has been extraordinary.

Liz Phair: The industry saw their revenue threatened by streaming and file sharing. Women had been doing the damn thing for most of the '90s. It wasn't Lilith Fair era, but Lilith Fair was recognizing the fact that the industry sort of shut down the woman thing. They're like, "Okay, we've done that." And then they were just going to arbitrarily shut it down. And there was this sense of, "Well, you don't actually draw tickets, you don't actually sell tickets." It's like the female sports thing, where you don't put the bodies in the seat. That era, the way I interpreted that, and I don't know if this is a lucky break or if it was a situation that pushed me into the choices I made, but I was a young mother at that point. So I was like, "Yeah, I'm watching *Blue's Clues*." Like, "Something serious happening out there. I'm watching

Blue's Clues. And he's awesome. His songs are great." There was always, though—and I feel like Shirley [Manson] is speaking to this—I can remember the time my management came in and sat me down. It must have been 2003. They said, "If you want to continue this lifestyle, you're going to have to have five different jobs, five different revenue streams. The artist, as such, is over; being an artist and everything poking out from that." Which to me was like, "That's the digital moment right there," because it was just instantly clear that because things didn't have to happen in person anymore—MTV had accelerated that—to be a part of that culture was going to be possible for people without leaving their home. And I think that was on the horizon, or it was already there. Picture a river. I'm trying to think of the Mississippi or something, a river that's very heavily invested in industry. The river flows this way, and we take all our goods down this way, whatever. The digital revolution was completely reversing the flow. And now instead of, "We are going to stage something somewhere that everyone's going to drive a billion miles to come see," that was going to be reversed, and everyone was going to have access to anyone that the labels put up through these new revenue streams, which was going to change everything. And it did. It was an intense shift. But again, I didn't see it as fan forced. I saw it as industry forced.

Melissa Auf der Maur: I started becoming comfortable as a front person. That was hard to do. I was a bass player for many reasons, but fronting my own band was exciting and great. Because I signed my first record to Capitol Records, the second record had quite a great budget related to it, and I always made my records very affordable with friends and never spent a ton of money, so I got to make what I'm most proud of, which is *Out of*

Our Minds, which is also when I fell in love with Tony Stone, who is my husband and cofounder of Basilica Hudson. The last eight years of my life have been devoted to a reclaiming this 1880s factory that gives a voice to independence and innovative voices in all forms, whether it's environmental advocates or a musician or a writer and filmmakers. We focus on music and film a lot.

It was during the making of my second record that I fell in love with Tony Stone. I had also moved back to Montreal because I was really done with this country. It was after the Iraq War, so 9/11 had already kind of made things pretty sad, and then the Iraq War was, like—the Montrealer in me just could not accept the political landscape. It was during the Bush era. So I moved back to Montreal, but then I fell in love with a New Yorker, and love is more important than politics. I wanted to be with him, and we moved here to Hudson, New York, because it was a geographical in-between of New York City and Montreal.

I released *Out of Our Minds* with a really interesting women-run company in Montreal called the PHI Centre, run by a very eccentric, interesting person, Phoebe Greenberg. I met her at Sundance [Film Festival] because Tony and I made a film that accompanied the album. Capitol Records looked at me and said, "Are you making a record?" And I was like, "No, I'm making a concept record. There's a film. There's a comic book. We're going to bring it to movie theaters, art galleries," and they were like, "That sounds complicated." That was a moment where I was ahead of my time. Next thing you know, two years later, every musician needs to make a movie, needs to make a book or whatever. Capitol didn't understand; they were staring at me. I'm like, "No, it's a whole package, and you have to like multimedia." And I don't even like the internet, but it was like literally multimedia that could be distributed in all these ways.

The last show I played for my second solo record, which is pretty much the last full show I played, was in August of 2011. My daughter was born in October 2011. It was a metal festival in Toronto called Heavy TO. I was eight months pregnant, and I was the only woman on the bill with Mastodon, Slayer, Rob Zombie, Judas Priest, and I was like, "This is the perfect way to go. I'm done."

I happily dove into motherhood. I did like a real, real intensive motherhood. No babysitters: my mother's not here; Tony's parents are not around much either. So I was a full-time mother. I had never been home for a year straight, and I breastfed for multiple years, and I just gave my daughter nothing but a simple, warm, tiny little town life. I walked the streets of this town more than—I mean, I had never lived anywhere for more than six months in my life, so by the time I was forty, and with my daughter here in Hudson, I had never owned a house, I had never even really learned how to cook or clean. No domestic ability. I'm still learning. It's really hard to always basically live like a teenager in a rock band and then become a mother. So it's been a hard learning curve, but I'm eight years in—she just turned seven. And so, my process really started, you know, once I got pregnant, I was like, "That's it. I'm changing my life. I'm going to understand the other side of this."

I MOVED FROM THE LIBERAL BUBBLE OF WESTERN MASSACHUSETTS to central Indiana in June of 2024 for a full-time teaching job. Before I left, I was able to attend a talk by the renowned Marxist feminist professor and author Silvia Federici. I'd become a huge fan of Federici's book *Caliban and the Witch* and the follow-up, *Witches, Witch-Hunting, and Women*. The latter is a condensed, simplified version of the main themes in *Caliban*. Federici investigates violence against women as having occurred alongside capitalist expansion. She examines the root causes and consequences for women; presents the processes of enclosure, (land) dispossession, expropriation; and, finally, addresses present-day witch hunts and their role in the expansion of capitalist accumulation.

I found compelling comparisons between sixteenth- and seventeenth-century witch hunts and the treatment of women during the war on terror. Specific groups and types of behavior are targeted during moments of historical change. Persecutions are typical during these moments, and the witch hunts played a major role during the Great Transformation, which was fundamental in creating a capitalist society.[2] The kinds of women who were targeted were outcasts. Vagrants. Women who were independent, self-sufficient; enslaved women; women who owned property or didn't attend church regularly. Accusations of witchcraft occurred at a pivotal moment in Colonial New England, for example: the transition from a communal, agrarian society to a mercantile economic system brought with it the development of sexual divisions of labor. This is not to say that women's work and men's work didn't exist before capitalism, but through the processes of colonization and the development of capitalism, we've been burdened with strict binary systems that dictate women's work and men's work. By that time, pseudoscience had already codified sexual differences, so of course women would stay at home and men would participate in the public sphere, outside the home. Arbitrary distinctions between femininity and masculinity grew out of the continuing development of a global capitalist economy, and sexism has been sewn into the very fabric of our national identity. So of course it exists in our institutions and cultural understandings.

The music industry follows the same blueprint: it is racially and sexually segregated by design. It is not the by-product of an unfortunate series of accidents or coincidences. Women need to be the "other." Black artists can be foremothers, forefathers, and progenitors of the rock genre, but integration would mean dismantling the foundation of a corporate industry whose existence rests on the falsehood that rock and roll is white, male, and phallic. The lasting impact in terms of the legacy of alternative music in the 1990s is the ideological devaluation of women and the devaluation of their creativity, despite the fact that women were critical and commercial successes. Three decades later, I can stand in front of a class of thirty college students, and not one of them has heard of any of the bands interviewed for this book.

Monopolization and privatization of the music industry necessitate strict regulation of women's creative reproduction because it is a capitalist enterprise, and capitalism depends on the maintenance of gender hierarchies. Alt-rock women in the 1990s were outspoken, they were feminists, they looked weird, they were loud and independent, they were messy; they wrote music for women and subverted the male gaze. They incited a moral panic. Ultimately, they were accused of emasculating American men to the point that the country was left vulnerable to a terrorist attack on its own soil. After their excommunication from the industry, some women changed careers and started families. Some continued to create and make music without access to an audience and outside of the mainstream rock economy. But working outside of that enclosed, corporate framework meant that their labor was not valued or visible, and it lost its place in broader historical memory. In a newly consolidated corporate media landscape, rendering these women invisible was akin to burning them at the stake.

EPILOGUE: WE'RE TAKING BACK THE NARRATIVE

I remember this one article would always pop up from East Coast Rocker, or something. It was like, "L7, some tough bitches," and that was the headline of this article. And that was the only thing that was coming up. And it was just, like, really? Is that our fucking legacy? So I kind of feel like we're taking back the narrative a little bit.

—Donita Sparks, L7

INTERVIEWED DONITA SPARKS IN JULY 2015 AT HER OFFICE SPACE in Santa Monica. It was my second trip to the West Coast, my fifth Women of Rock Oral History Project interview, and the first time I came close to vomiting due to nerves. I've almost thrown up twice since: once in a hotel room with Cindy Wilson of the B-52s, and once in an elevator with Shirley Manson. I entered a small, carpeted room with my videographer, Sophia, and noted a potted plant and an open window, just in case. There were people in an adjoining room, studiously working on laptops, editing video. I found out later that they were working on *Pretend We're Dead*, the L7 documentary released in 2017, spearheaded by Sparks, to preserve the band's legacy in the wake of historical obsolescence.

During the interview, Sparks discussed women's erasure from rock history and 1990s rock canon. Oddly enough, in 2014, we had both typed "L7" into our respective Google search engines with the same result—an article titled something like, "These Chicks Can Rock." Donita embarked on the documentary project, and I made business cards and started an oral history collection. She spoke candidly about her history, L7's formation and rise to success, the band's subsequent demise in 2001, and L7's re-formation in 2014. She discussed legacy and how it's easier to be remembered when you have some capital—or a good publicist. Without financial backing, it's easy for bands like L7, who existed before the advent of household internet, but who were major players in their respective scenes, to get lost in a "grunge" narrative predicated in a false history made up mostly of men in flannel shirts, sprinkled with a handful of female figureheads, for taste.

I'm a hippie at heart, and I believe in divine guidance, cosmic coincidence, and that things generally happen when they're supposed to. In 2015, "soft grunge" was a popular aesthetic in the bucolic college town I'd been living in since 2013. It gained traction on Tumblr (RIP), television, and magazines. College girls played in bands again, and these bands sounded like they had been birthed from the atrophied vagina of the '90s. Something was percolating beneath the surface. As I continued to conduct interviews with rock icons, I learned that many of

them had reconnected, had re-formed their bands, were scheduling tours, or were recording new material. I conducted my
interview with Nina Gordon and Louise Post at Brad Wood's
studio. I went to the bathroom and urinated next to Liz Phair's
Exile in Guyville gold record (Wood recorded and produced it)
and reentered the room to Nina and Louise recording vocals
for what would be their first Veruca Salt single in over fifteen
years. Nonconformist, alt-rock '90s women never went away;
they were pushed out of public consciousness by a predict-
able cultural and political shift. Their legacies suffered, too, as
we transitioned from analog into a fully digital age. Many of
the women in this book changed careers after their celebrity
faded; they went back to school, got married, raised children.
But many continued to create, albeit unobserved. Some people, like Sparks, resented the revisionist narrative propagated
in the years since the grunge/rock phenomenon and took it
upon themselves to document their own histories. What I had
sensed was percolating beneath the surface of dominant popular culture emerged as a full-on '90s rock revival.

Donita Sparks: I kind of feel like we're taking back the narrative a little bit on that, because, you know, there were others out there. There was a whole fleet of women playing music
in the '90s, you know? And to have two people be the spokespeople constantly is just, like, "What the fuck?" You know what
I mean? Can we get Kim Deal to chime in on something over
here, please?

And now all the young kids are finding out about us and
spreading it around and wearing our shirts and coming to our
shows. And I think it's very inspirational to them, because I've
heard from young people, like, "Wow, you guys, the '90s were so

amazing with all the women playing in rock bands, and all the all-female bands," like the all-female band has gone sort of—not extinct, but it's just not what it was back in the '90s.

And they should be pissed off about a lot of shit. So, you know, I think that they look to women of the '90s, and I think one of grunge's great legacies is the killing off of misogyny in rock for quite a while. It was very passé being misogynist in rock there for a while. So that was helped by the guys in Nirvana, and the guys in Pearl Jam, and bands like us, and Babes in Toyland and Lunachicks, and then riot grrrl later. So yeah, I think that's a big deal.

L7 RELEASED THEIR DOCUMENTARY FILM IN 2017 AND THEIR FIRST album in twenty years, *Scatter the Rats*, in 2019; Nina Gordon and Louise Post ended their fifteen-year feud, got the original Veruca Salt lineup back together, released *Ghost Notes* in 2015, and toured the globe. The year 2018 marked the twenty-fifth anniversary of Liz Phair's *Exile in Guyville*. Matador Records released a limited-edition box set, and Phair began touring. She released *Soberish*, her first album in eleven years, on Chrysalis Records in 2021. The Breeders released the album *All Nerve* in 2018, featuring the classic *Last Splash* lineup (the Deal sisters, Josephine Wiggs, and Jim MacPherson). Garbage released their latest album, *No Gods No Masters*, in 2021, and last summer, Shirley Manson gifted me tickets to the first concert I'd attended since this fucking pandemic started: Alanis Morissette, Garbage, and Cat Power. Together, they toured the United States in celebration of Morissette's album *Jagged Little Pill*, which had turned twenty-five. Courtney Love is publishing a memoir and finished recording a new solo album. Louise Post released her first solo album in April 2023, and the Breeders and Liz Phair embarked on their respective anniversary tours.

Nina Gordon: A year before I approached Louise about playing music again, we dissolved the Veruca Salt LLC. So for all those years we were apart, we still had a company together—we just never got around to it? We had people paying taxes for us, and we'd never dissolved the band. We'd never signed the papers that actually dissolved the band. So we finally got around to it. We were like, "We have got to break up this band." This was fifteen years later. "We have got to break up. This is ridiculous. We have got to break up the band." So, finally, we all signed the papers, and then a year later, this light bulb goes off that's like, "I want to play music with her again. Let's do it." And now we got the band back together. We had to form a new LLC—

Louise Post: So dumb, but we had to dismantle it down to nothing in order to re-form. When Nina and I got together and saw each other for the first time in fourteen years, we talked about playing music, and later that summer, I saw Steve and asked him if—I was down in San Diego and I had lunch with him—and I said, "If we were to get together and we were to try to play music again, would you be interested?" And he paused and said, "I've been wondering for years what my answer would be to this question, and it's yes. I didn't know what it would be, but it's yes." And I think he decided he wasn't going to play bass ever again, and he stuck to that for about ten years, or twelve years—strangely, like Jim—and I don't know about us and guitar, but everyone's better. Because we weren't done when we broke up, we weren't done creatively. Interpersonally, we fell apart, but our friendship also wasn't done; it was just an unfortunate occurrence of events that we couldn't hold it together and that we needed to break apart. We weren't done creatively as a band. I would guess Jim would say the same. He left, but part of him wishes he had stayed to make the next Veruca Salt record. It was his baby, too.

I'm proud of Nina and I for getting past our shit and getting back together and doing this now. And doing it as mothers and really living the dream. It's not like we have round-the-clock nannies and we're living in mansions and all of that stuff that one would imagine in Hollywood, the dream of LA or whatever, or in the industry, but we are living the most incredible dream I could have imagined. In making this album [*Ghost Notes*] together, having renewed our friendship and our children being friends and having Jim and Steve back in my life is such an incredible gift, and to know these people again who were like my family—as a child of a broken family, I think my biggest dream would be that everyone reunited, my parents reunited, my family reunited, and we were together again and there was a sense of harmony. And that was not meant to happen, but this was apparently meant to happen, and this was another family in my life. And beyond that, we have families of our own, and so this doesn't carry an unnecessary weight, an inappropriate weight, that it did back then. Now it can be in its proper place, and we can be musicians and work together and create together and have very fulfilled happy personal lives that we have cultivated over time with blood, sweat, and tears and love, and now it's just like a world of abundance. And you know, Nina and I can craft our futures together, independently, but we can work towards being songwriters and co-songwriters because we now know how to do that, and we work at that, too, for a long time to come. It feels like the world is our oyster and we can do whatever we want with it right now if we really honor what's been given to us and have gratitude for what's been given to us and what's in our present—we have an abundant future. I feel like we're at a beautiful juncture and a great place.

BABES IN TOYLAND NEVER DEVIATED FROM THEIR PUNK ROCK, do-it-yourself ethos and remained a band for over thirty years. They ignored pressures from major-label representatives and existed, in many ways, outside the churning wheels of the industry model.

Lori Barbero: For some people, success is money and being rich and famous. To me, success is going through your life, doing what you enjoy, and being able to live doing that. Even if you're eating ramen noodles for seven months because you toured and you didn't make any money, it's like, "Guess what I just did? I just traveled around the country and met so many cool people and saw these places and cities and old friends, met new friends." You can give me all the money in the world, and you can't replace that stuff. I think that we were very successful because we did what we wanted to do for thirty-five years.

A NEW GENERATION OF FANS IS DISCOVERING THESE PIONEERING women because of social media, because of their parents, and because a younger generation of pop stars are starting to give credit where credit is most certainly due. During the pandemic, Miley Cyrus went on a cover song spree during her backyard sessions, interpreting songs originally recorded by the Cranberries, Melanie, Blondie, Dolly Parton, Brenda Lee, Nancy Sinatra, and male artists like Metallica, Bob Dylan, and the Replacements. I watched her perform "Doll Parts" on *The Howard Stern Show* wearing a Wendy O. Williams T-shirt, and for three minutes, I felt hope for the future of our nation's kids; that they might indeed inhabit the skills needed to weed through industry-produced bullshit and uncover good music. Now more than ever, as a woman's right to determine her future rests precariously in the hands of an absurdly dysfunctional government (bad people on both sides!), we can look to the nuance, artistry, and activism of '90s rock women who most certainly changed the world when we needed it. In 2018, Melissa Auf der Maur honored her former bandmate Courtney Love at Basilica's first event honoring pioneering people. Michael Stipe, Chloë Sevigny, and other A-list celebs descended on a small town in upstate New York to honor the career and feminism of a woman who deserves that and so much more (ahem, Rock Hall).

Melissa Auf der Maur: I think that Courtney and I and everyone in our generation are only going to start making the impact now. I know that there were people whose lives we changed that were growing with us. But I think it was a very niche, alternative culture, and I feel like Courtney's radically strange celebrity— the widow and the tragedy and the drugs and the chaos—really overshadows the impact of that band and those songs and, therefore, my role in it, too. It's just like Hole is a side note to who Courtney is, which is why I wanted to do that event last honoring her. Because that's not fair. That music, those three albums, and that person being so ahead of her time, and so fearless, and that's the only way that women could have been saying that at that time. Nobody was listening to any woman. We were all blind to how unbelievably not free we yet were.

My mother was only a second-wave feminist, and she's still alive. I mean, this just started. So I think it made a deep cultural impact with us. But it's those fifteen- and sixteen-year-old girls that we played with last month, that I think now is when we might see what our legacy might be because now there is a new world of people that have been raised in this corporate climate— you know, where are the real voices? Where is truth and individuality? And not these mass-consumed and created—not to mention completely illegal, corrupt, horrible—systems that are destroying our planet and destroying the people who live on it. And I don't mean just with environmental disasters but, like, the health care that we don't have that—just killing people, killing people for their own corporate advantages and greed, et cetera.

I think that it's the new youth who are going to discover real voices that were saying really ballsy things that are still needing to be said. So I think those girls are going to tap into where Hole fits. And as far as me beyond Hole—because I'm not just my five years in Hole—I think my legacy in rock music is that I'm happy that I've made a mark because it's given me so much and I love music. It's my favorite form of expression and my favorite way to share time with people. I'm happy I made an impact, but I have a lot of other worlds that I want to make impacts in.

IN 2021, FIONA APPLE, BIG THIEF, PHOEBE BRIDGERS, HAIM, Brittany Howard, and Grace Potter were the nominees for Best Rock Performance at the 2021 Grammy Awards. For the first time in industry history, the category was female dominated. Apple won for her song "Shameika" and took home the award for Best Alternative Music Album. In June 2021, Olivia Rodrigo announced her *Sour Prom* concert film, with a photo of her as a mascara-streaked, Gen Z Carrie, wearing a tiara, and holding a bouquet of roses, an image directly referencing the *Live Through This* album cover. She performed Veruca Salt's 1994 hit "Seether" during her Sour Tour. Doja Cat released a hyperproduced interpretation of Hole's 1998 single "Celebrity Skin." Young fans took to the internet in droves, bestowing praise and admiration upon Doja Cat for going "pop punk" without realizing it was a cover. However, Love's poignant lyrics about the pitfalls of fame were exchanged in favor of safer, more benign, replacements. Instead "A walking study in demonology," Doja Cat sings, "A walking fire, you can't get rid of me" and the word *sluts* is replaced with *trash*. This is one of the reasons this book is important and why we need to look back, give credit where credit is due, and acknowledge the revolutionary work of '90s rock women. But we also need to take a hard look at where we are right now; for all the supposed freedom we have as women and artists, Doja Cat can't even say the word *slut* in a twenty-first-century rock song. What does that say about our moment? As a culture, we've embraced a commercially viable type of feminism, American feminism. It's the brand of feminism that equates nudity and sex with personal freedom. If people want to expose themselves in public, if that's empowering to them, that's wonderful. I adore Lizzo and relish her twerking, flute-playing, "big girl" ass.

What disturbs me is this is the only feminism visible in pop culture today. No one is subverting the male gaze dressed in a leotard and twirling on a stripper pole. There's a lack of self-awareness and cultural critique, and there's a deficit in the educated irreverence inherent in 1990s alternative music. Amyl and the Sniffers has it. Otoboke Beaver has it. Wet Leg has it. It was gloriously bizarre to see these indie/pop/faerie geeks at the 2022 Grammy Awards performing a two-minute song about a couch, in front of Beyoncé and Taylor Swift. The band looked completely alone as they collected their awards, and months later, I can't help but wonder where the momentum is. In the '90s, award ceremonies looked like high school cafeterias; there were the popular kids—the pop stars—and the alternative outcasts and interlopers. Alternative culture, meaning invisible or alternative to music considered viable in the market, has receded back into the underground, where there is a surplus of politically relevant, intelligent, feminist bands, but my focus in this book is the mainstream. If college radio hadn't existed, if MTV hadn't played music videos highlighting indie and alternative bands, if my local radio station hadn't promoted those women, hadn't interviewed them, and offered free tickets to their shows; if chain stores hadn't sold these records, if *Rolling Stone* hadn't put Liz Phair or Courtney Love or Shirley Manson on its covers, it is unlikely that I would have had the tools or the access to discover the wealth of women in rock on my own. Like I said, immature, nerd, oldest child, lived in the suburbs.

Olivia Rodrigo has hailed 1990s alternative rock artists as core influences on her second album, *GUTS*. Apparently, when she was a teenager, her mother would wake her up each morning to Babes in Toyland's *Fontanelle*; nice work, Mom. Now Rodrigo is doing the work that Nirvana did in the early '90s: she's talking about the women who inspired her; she's covering their songs, live, in arenas; she's referencing them in interviews; and now she's performing alongside them. She invited the Breeders to open for her at Madison Square Garden in 2024. I logged on to Instagram after confirming with Josephine Wiggs (and half-heartedly trying to score some tickets for my niece), and Rodrigo even showed up to see the band at their show in Los Angeles. In the words of Josephine, "We thought, this is a weird combo, but it's cool and it'll expose us to the young'uns." Indeed. My twelve-year-old niece wears Nirvana sweatshirts—my college students, too—and H&M sells Smashing Pumpkins and Hole T-shirts. It takes everything in my power not to scream, "NAME ONE SONG!" at fourteen-year-olds on the street.

The wave of women in rock and alternative music in the 1990s was a hugely important moment in music history and also in the history of the United States as a whole. The mainstream supported dissenting women who disrupted convention, and the industry discovered that anti-sexism was commercially viable. It was a great moment for young people—and all revolutionary moments have been youth centered and led—because, in the words of the late, great bell hooks, feminism is for everybody. Everyone benefits. The consequences alt-rock women experienced at the end of the decade is relevant to the consequences women are currently facing. The institutional and political conservatism that generated backlash against women's progress—in the late '90s and again during the Trump era—is reflected in the lack of diversity in mainstream rock and alternative categories today. There is a direct correlation between media consolidation, privatization, and conservatism, and the negative impacts on women—and in terms of the music industry—on their creative reproduction. After 9/11, economic and political changes promoted in a consolidated media produced a realignment of social priorities, norms, and values. Dissenting women were silenced, and transgressive forms of femininity were replaced with sexier, hegemonic ideals. Another correlation can be made between the privatization of the music industry, the regulation of women's artistic output, and the regulation of women's sexuality and reproductive capacity. State control is a condition for the construction of stringent forms of social control. In 1991, alt-rock women protested antiabortion laws, and the Gulf War, live. They toured and were able to make money as underground musicians because Live Nation didn't own every fucking venue in the United States. Streaming didn't exist, and fans bought albums on tape or CD. MTV promoted independent artists.

In 1996, regulations that protected media from being monopolized by corporations were removed by Bill Clinton. College radio disappeared, Clear Channel instituted a gender quota, and by the end of the decade, women couldn't get played on the radio. After 9/11, Clear Channel promoted jingoism, deciding for themselves which songs were appropriate for the postwar American public, effectively condemning dissent. This restructuring was paired with a state-sponsored politics of fear: in the early 2000s, a daily, color-coded alert system warned Americans how close we were to another terrorist attack; the Patriot Act expanded law enforcement's surveillance powers; since 9/11, the US has been perpetually at war, fighting terrorism overseas. Security is ubiquitous when we travel—log on to the internet or social media, attend events, drive—hell, even while walking.

This fear of the "other"—of brown people, of Muslims, and of feminists—emerged in the mainstream in many ways, one of which was the return to traditional musical archetypes and gendered divisions of labor within the industry. Sexy pop stars, seductive boy bands, and nostalgic, beer-drinking, drug-taking, guitar-slinging, indie rock men. Men could be weird (Marilyn Manson), aggressive (Limp Bizkit), or toe the line into the new millennium (Pearl Jam), but not a single woman mentioned in this book survived the cultural and political shifts—unless they completely changed (Liz Phair). I don't think this is a coincidence.

The lack of nonconformity and dissent in mainstream music today is structural. There are no longer careers to be had or money to be made. You're either a viral superstar forced to work within a certain framework and with a handful of producers, or you're a broke-ass independent musician. For fans, manufactured convenience has taken over. It's not that people prefer convenience. It's easy to install an app and click on a song you like. It's harder to find a store that sells hard copies of albums and then to shell out forty dollars for a vinyl record. We have elected people to govern us, Republicans and Democrats, who have created this choiceless reality we find ourselves in. Amazon and Microsoft received military contracts to help with drone programs, and Spotify invests in weapons manufacturing—basically, shopping online and listening to music on an app directly supports the military-industrial complex.

And you might be asking, "What does this have to do with women? Or women in rock?" I teach women's and gender studies, and I'm constantly reminding my students to think intersectionally. People have unique identities and lived experiences, which means their experiences are shaped by their race, sexuality, politics, the economy, culture, and religion, for example, in different ways. Removing regulations and allowing corporations to subsume independent and college radio stations negatively affected women more than men. Allowing major record labels to absorb smaller, independent labels negatively affected women. After 9/11, when the industry promoted the Bush administration's politics of fear, dissenting women were punished. Dissenting men got a pass. Patriotism, like masculinity, is an ideology that suggests specific beliefs and behaviors are best or for the good of the nation. It is antiradical, heroic, and militaristic. Men could be critical of Bush or the war in Iraq (see: Neil

Young, Kanye, Willie Nelson, Pearl Jam) because of their gender. Women had to navigate an industry and a culture in which they found themselves suspect by virtue of their gender—in part due to the overwhelming, and dangerous, influence of third-wave feminism in the 1990s.

We can use music as a lens to investigate the history of feminism in the United States. We can use the subjective experiences of women in rock in the 1990s to think beyond parity in an inherently patriarchal institution. We can build something new, collectively. It's my hope that by looking back at this revolutionary moment, we'll be emboldened to think again about how we might embody real change.

ACKNOWLEDGMENTS

MANY PEOPLE CONTRIBUTED TO THE COMPLETION OF THIS BOOK, and while I may never be able to repay everyone who has tolerated me throughout this long journey, I hope that recognizing that tolerance will suffice! Thank you to my ball and chain, Meg Martin, for your unwavering support, for calling me a genius when we both know I'm not, and for always encouraging me. I look forward to being slightly less stressed and spending more time together.

Thank you to my literary agent, Elias Altman. I'm so grateful you responded to my email query. You're stuck with me.

Thank you, Ben Schafer, Cisca Schreefel, Julie Ford, and everyone at Hachette Books and Grand Central. This is a long, hard process, but you made it easy.

Thank you, Meryl Fingrutd, for keeping me sane and encouraging me when I'm frustrated or simply not feeling up to the task. It's been a pleasure having you in my corner!

I am grateful for my family: Kyla Schmigle, Bianca Roderick, Cade Jones, Mom (Meg Jones), Dad (Carl Pearson); my brothers and sister-in-law, Sean Schmigle, Amanda Jones-Pearson, and Mike Roderick, for reading my work, supporting me, and encouraging me. Thank you Kathy Schmigle for looking over contracts and for my inspirational mug.

I am madly in love with my nieces and nephews, Everly, Hudson, Cash, and Margo. FaceTiming you kids is one of my favorite pastimes and instantly gets me out of any funk I find myself in.

I have to thank my Smith College family who sculpted me into the confident, insufferable woman I am today. Steve Waksman (the REAL Doctor of Rock), Susan Van Dyne, Debra Carney, Sid Dalby, Erika Laquer, Debbie Richards, Beth Myers, and the Special Collections staff, THANK YOU.

And a special thanks to my Ball State University community—particularly Sharon Jones, Elizabeth Agnew, Pat Collier, and Rachael Smith. Thank you for making my transition a smooth one and for your constant encouragement during my doctoral journey.

I am forever indebted to Dr. Christian Appy, Dr. Joel Wolfe, Dr. Daniel Czitrom, and Dr. Kelly Anderson. Your time, expertise, and encouragement over the years have not gone unnoticed. I respect you all as scholars and as human beings, and I appreciate your taking me under your wing. Special thanks to Mary Lashway for always knowing what the hell is going on.

Thank you, Gianna LaMorte, Casey Kittrell, Jessica Hopper, Evelyn McDonnell, and everyone at University of Texas Press for giving me my big break.

Finally, I would like to thank my friends: Alex Fullerton for loving dogs and funding our road trips and mini-vacations; Sean Donovan and Crystal Ford for being the best pals and bandmates; Piper Preston, Jen Dessinger, Sophia Cacciola, and Michael J. Epstein for traveling around with me, recording, and editing interviews for zero dollars.

To my Falmouth recovery family, thank you for changing my life: Bill D., Kathy B., Frank, Mary, Meg, Douglas, Erika, Brandi, Bree, Marilyn Fox, and all my bagel girls—THANK YOU.

To my Muncie family—Pam and Brian Johnson, Buck, Chuck, Annie, JR, JJ, Ariella, Taylor, Lizzie, Cope, Colton, Devon, and Gage.

Adele Bertei, Lydia Lunch, Marianne Faithfull, Cynthia Ross, Jill Emery, Honeychild Coleman, Chan Marshall, Josephine Wiggs, Alice Bag, and JD Samson—thanks for starting out as interviewees and becoming friends.

BIBLIOGRAPHY

Adams, Don, and Arlene Goldbard. "New Deal Cultural Programs: Experiments in Cultural Democracy." Webster's World of Cultural Democracy. http://www.wwcd.org/policy/US/newdeal.html.

Adorno, Theodor W. "On Popular Music." In *Culture Theory and Popular Culture*, edited by John Storkey, 197–209. Athens: University of Georgia Press, 1998.

Appy, Christian G. *Working-Class War*. Chapel Hill: University of North Carolina Press, 1993.

Arnold, Gina. "Bricks Are Heavy." *Entertainment Weekly*, June 19, 1992. https://ew.com/article/1992/06/19/bricks-are-heavy/.

Arundel, Jim. "Belly: Colonic Youth." *Melody Maker*, July 4, 1992. Rock's Backpages. Accessed March 31, 2023. https://www.rocksbackpages.com/Library/Article/belly-colonic-youth.

Battersby, Christine. *Gender and Genius: Towards a Feminist Aesthetics*. London: Women's Press, 1989.

Baumgardner, Jennifer, and Amy Richards. *Manifesta: Young Women, Feminism, and the Future*. New York: Farrar, Straus and Giroux, 2000.

Benincasa, Sara. "I Worked at Woodstock '99." Medium. August 4, 2021. https://sarajbenincasa.medium.com/i-worked-at-woodstock-99-7d8ff58f0859.

Bennett, Judith M. "The Patriarchal Equilibrium." In *History Matters: Patriarchy and the Challenge of Feminism*, 54–81. Philadelphia: University of Pennsylvania Press, 2007.

Bohlman, Philip V. "Epilogue: Musics and Canons." In *Disciplining Music: Musicology and Its Canons*, edited by Katherine Bergeron and Philip V. Bohlman, 197–210. Chicago: University of Chicago Press, 1992.

Bowers, Jane M. "Feminist Scholarship and the Field of Musicology: II." *College Music Symposium* 30, no. 1 (Spring 1990): 1–13.

Brannigan, Paul. "'I Had All This Anger Bubbling Up Inside Me': Olivia Rodrigo Hails the Righteous Fury of Babes in Toyland and Rage Against the Machine as Core Influences on New Album Guts." Louder.

September 13, 2023. https://www.loudersound.com/news/olivia-rodrigo-babes-in-toyland-and-rage-against-the-machine.

Citron, Marcia J. *Gender and the Musical Canon*. Cambridge, England: University of Cambridge Press, 1993.

Crenshaw, Kimberlé W. "Demarginalizing the Intersection of Race and Sex: A Black Feminist Critique of Antidiscrimination Doctrine, Feminist Theory and Antiracist Politics." *University of Chicago Legal Forum* 1989, no. 1 (1989): 139–166.

Currie, James R. *Music and the Politics of Negation*. Bloomington: Indiana University Press, 2012.

Dalton, Stephen. "Throwing Muses: Serious Shrinking!" *New Musical Express*, February 2, 1991. Rock's Backpages. Accessed March 31, 2023. https://www.rocksbackpages.com/Library/Article/throwing-muses-serious-shrinking.

Davies, Helen. "All Rock and Roll Is Homosocial: The Representation of Women in the British Rock Music Press." *Popular Music* 20 (2001): 301–319.

Dijkstra, Bram. *Evil Sisters: The Threat of Female Sexuality and the Cult of Manhood*. New York: Alfred A. Knopf, 1996.

Dowling, Stephen. "Napster Turns 20: How It Changed the Music Industry." BBC. February 24, 2022. https://www.bbc.com/culture/article/20190531-napster-turns-20-how-it-changed-the-music-industry.

Edes, Alyssa. "Liz Phair on Demanding a Voice in 25 Years of 'Guyville.'" NPR. May 3, 2018. https://www.npr.org/2018/05/03/607116940/liz-phair-on-demanding-a-voice-in-25-years-of-guyville.

Faludi, Susan. *Backlash: Undeclared War Against Women*. London: Vintage, 1992.

———. *The Terror Dream: Fear and Fantasy in Post-9/11 America*. New York: Metropolitan Books, 2007.

Federici, Silvia. *Caliban and the Witch: Women, the Body and Primitive Accumulation*. London: Penguin, 2021.

———. *Witches, Witch-Hunting, and Women*. Oakland, CA: PM Press, 2018.

"50 Ways to Be a Feminist." *Ms.*, July 1994.

Guillory, John. *Cultural Capital: The Problem of Literary Canon Formation*. Chicago: University of Chicago Press, 1993.

Harvey, David. *A Brief History of Neoliberalism*. Oxford, England: Oxford University Press, 2007.

Haslam, Dave. "Courtney Love in Liverpool: The Scousers Who Taught the Grunge Icon How to Rock." *Guardian*, May 25, 2020. https://www.theguardian.com/music/2020/may/25/courtney-love-in-liverpool-scousers-wild-child-how-to-rock.

Herman, Edward S., and Noam Chomsky. *Manufacturing Consent: The Political Economy of the Mass Media*. London: Vintage Digital, 2010.

hooks, bell. *Feminist Theory: From Margin to Center*. Cambridge, MA: South End Press, 2000.

Hoskyns, Barney. "Angry Young Women." *Vogue*, 1991. Rock's Backpages. Accessed March 31, 2023. https://www.rocksbackpages.com/Library/Article /angry-young-women.

Klein, Naomi. *The Shock Doctrine: The Rise of Disaster Capitalism*. London: Penguin, 2014.

Lederman, Marsha. "Sarah McLachlan Says Lilith Fair Is Over." *Globe and Mail*, March 8, 2011. https://www.theglobeandmail.com/arts/music/sarah -mclachlan-says-lilith-fair-is-over/article569791.

Leonard, Marion. *Gender in the Music Industry: Rock, Discourse and Girl Power*. London: Routledge, 2017.

Lipsitz, G. *Time Passages: Collective Memory and American Popular Culture*. Minneapolis: University of Minnesota Press, 1990.

Lyons, James. *Selling Seattle: Representing Contemporary Urban America*. London: Wallflower, 2004.

May, Elaine Tyler. *Homeward Bound: American Families in the Cold War Era*. New York: Basic Books, 2017.

McClary, Susan. *Feminine Endings: Music, Gender & Sexuality*. Minneapolis: University of Minnesota Press, 1991.

Peisner, David. "Let It Bleed: The Oral History of PJ Harvey's 'Rid of Me.'" *SPIN*, March 31, 2015. https://www.spin.com/2013/05/pj-harvey-rid -of-me-oral-history-steve-albini/.

Peraino, Judith. "PJ Harvey's 'Man-Size Sextet' and the Inaccessible, Inescapable Gender." *Women and Music: A Journal of Gender and Culture* 2 (1998): 47–63.

Poirot, K. "Domesticating the Liberated Woman: Containment Rhetorics of Second Wave Radical/Lesbian Feminism." *Women's Studies in Communication* 32 (2009): 263–292.

Reddington, H. *The Lost Women of Rock Music: Female Musicians of the Punk Era*. Aldershot, England: Ashgate, 2007.

Saunders, Frances Stonor. *The Cultural Cold War: The CIA and the World of Arts and Letters*. New York: New Press, 2000.

Scherzinger, Martin. "Music, Corporate Power, and Unending War." *Cultural Critique*, no. 60 (2005): 23–67.

Schilt, Kristin. "'A Little Too Ironic': The Appropriation and Packaging of Riot Grrrl Politics by Mainstream Female Musicians." *Popular Music and Society* 26, no. 1 (2003): 5–16.

Scott, Joan Wallach. "The Problem of Invisibility." In *Retrieving Women's History: Changing Perceptions of the Role of Women in Politics and Society*, edited by S. Jay Kleinberg, 5–29. London: Berg/Unesco, 1988.

Strong, Catherine. *Grunge: Music and Memory*. Aldershot, England: Ashgate, 2011.

———. "Grunge, Riot Grrrl, and the Forgetting of Women in Popular Culture." *Journal of Popular Culture* 44, no. 2 (2011): 398–416.

———. "Shaping the Past of Popular Music: Memory, Forgetting and Documenting." *The SAGE Handbook of Popular Music*, edited by Andy Bennett and Steve Waksman, 419–433. Los Angeles: SAGE, 2015.

"10 Essential Major Label Debuts from Indie Artists: Sonic Youth-Goo." Treble. January 28, 2022. https://www.treblezine.com/10-essential-major-label-debuts-from-indie-artists/.

"The 300 Best Albums of the Past 30 Years (1985–2014)." *SPIN*, September 1, 2016. https://www.spin.com/2015/05/the-300-best-albums-of-the-past-30-years-1985-2014/.

"The Time Magazine Vault." *Time*. Accessed December 10, 2023. https://time.com/vault/subject/gender/.

"The Top 11 Hottest Women in Grunge." *SF Weekly*, September 22, 2011. https://www.sfweekly.com/music/the-top-11-hottest-women-in-grunge/article_df224d40-0ca0-5730-a697-3a52c3adf233.html.

Tucker, Sherrie. *Swing Shift: "All-Girl" Bands of the 1940s*. Durham, NC: Duke University Press, 2001.

Unsworth, Cathi. "L7: Babes In Boyland." *Melody Maker*, August 29, 1992. Rock's Backpages. Accessed March 31, 2023. https://www.rocksback pages.com/Library/Article/l7-babes-in-boyland.

Wald, Gayle. "Just a Girl? Rock Music, Feminism, and the Cultural Construction of Female Youth." *Signs* 23, no. 3 (1998): 585–610. http://www.jstor.org/stable/3175302.

Weisbard, Eric. "Veruca Salt: *American Thighs* (Minty Fresh)." *SPIN*, November 1994. Rock's Backpages. Accessed March 31, 2023. https://www.rocksbackpages.com/Library/Article/veruca-salt-iamerican-thighsi-minty-fresh.

Whiteley, Sheila. *Women and Popular Music: Sexuality, Identity and Subjectivity*. London: Routledge, 2000.

Wood, Ellen Meiksins. *Democracy Against Capitalism: Renewing Historical Materialism*. Brooklyn: Verso, 2016.

Wurtzel, Elizabeth. "Girl Trouble." *New Yorker*, June 22, 1992. https://www.newyorker.com/magazine/1992/06/29/girl-trouble.

Yarm, Mark. "'Going Out of Business Since 1988!': An Oral History of Sub Pop Records." Northwest Passage. Accessed March 31, 2023. http://www.revolutioncomeandgone.com/articles/7/sub-pop-history.php.

NOTES

Introduction

1. Shirley Manson, Women of Rock Oral History Project interview with the author, 2018.
2. The festival was revived once in 2010. Marsha Lederman, "Sarah McLachlan Says Lilith Fair Is Over," *Globe and Mail*, March 8, 2011, https://www.theglobeandmail.com/arts/music/sarah-mclachlan-says-lilith-fair-is-over/article569791.
3. Susan Faludi, *The Terror Dream: Fear and Fantasy in Post-9/11 America* (New York: Metropolitan Books, 2007).

Chapter 1: Fast and Frightening

1. I wore the same outfit to my parents' wedding the year before.
2. Paul Brannigan, "'I Had All This Anger Bubbling Up Inside Me': Olivia Rodrigo Hails the Righteous Fury of Babes in Toyland and Rage Against the Machine as Core Influences on New Album Guts," Louder, September 13, 2023, https://www.loudersound.com/news/olivia-rodrigo-babes-in-toyland-and-rage-against-the-machine.
3. James Lyons, *Selling Seattle: Representing Contemporary Urban America* (London: Wallflower, 2004), 120.
4. Lyons, *Selling Seattle*, 121.
5. On structural racism (in the music industry): David Bruenger, *Making Money, Making Music: History and Core Concepts* (Berkeley: University of California Press, 2016), 105–108; Kimberlé W. Crenshaw, "Demarginalizing the Intersection of Race and Sex: A Black Feminist Critique of Antidiscrimination Doctrine, Feminist Theory and Antiracist Politics," *University of Chicago Legal Forum* 1989, no. 1 (1989): 139–166; Angela Davis, *Blues Legacies and Black Feminism* (New York: Vintage, 1998); Matthew D. Morrison, "Race, Blacksound, and the (Re)Making of Musicological Discourse," *Journal of the American Musicological Society* 72, no. 3 (December 1, 2019): 781–823.

Chapter 2: The Whole Industry Descended on Us

1. Alyssa Edes, "Liz Phair on Demanding a Voice in 25 Years of 'Guyville,'" NPR, May 3, 2018, https://www.npr.org/2018/05/03/607116940/liz-phair-on-demanding-a-voice-in-25-years-of-guyville.

Chapter 3: The Hard Thing Was Always the Press

1. Barney Hoskyns, "Angry Young Women," *Vogue*, 1991, Rock's Backpages, accessed March 31, 2023, https://www.rocksbackpages.com/Library/Article/angry-young-women.

2. "The Top 11 Hottest Women in Grunge," *SF Weekly*, September 22, 2011, https://www.sfweekly.com/music/the-top-11-hottest-women-in-grunge/article_df224d40-0ca0-5730-a697-3a52c3adf233.html.

3. Stephen Dalton, "Throwing Muses: Serious Shrinking!," *New Musical Express*, February 2 1991, Rock's Backpages, accessed March 31, 2023, https://www.rocksbackpages.com/Library/Article/throwing-muses-serious-shrinking.

4. Jim Arundel, "Belly: Colonic Youth," *Melody Maker*, July 4, 1992, Rock's Backpages, accessed March 31, 2023, https://www.rocksbackpages.com/Library/Article/belly-colonic-youth.

5. Eric Weisbard, "Veruca Salt: *American Thighs* (Minty Fresh)," *SPIN*, November 1994, Rock's Backpages, accessed March 31, 2023, https://www.rocksbackpages.com/Library/Article/veruca-salt-iamerican-thighsi-minty-fresh.

6. Alyssa Edes, "Liz Phair on Demanding a Voice in 25 Years of 'Guyville,'" NPR, May 3, 2018, https://www.npr.org/2018/05/03/607116940/liz-phair-on-demanding-a-voice-in-25-years-of-guyville.

7. "50 Ways to Be a Feminist," *Ms.*, July 1994.

8. K. Poirot, "Domesticating the Liberated Woman: Containment Rhetorics of Second Wave Radical/Lesbian Feminism." *Women's Studies in Communication* 32 (2009): 263–292.

9. Catherine Strong, *Grunge: Music and Memory* (Aldershot, England: Ashgate, 2011).

10. Strong, *Grunge*.

11. Helen Davies, "All Rock and Roll Is Homosocial: The Representation of Women in the British Rock Music Press," *Popular Music* 20 (2001): 301–319.

Chapter 4: Before We Knew It, We Were Topping the Charts

1. "10 Essential Major Label Debuts from Indie Artists: Sonic Youth-Goo," Treble, January 28, 2022, https://www.treblezine.com/10-essential-major-label-debuts-from-indie-artists/.

Chapter 5: Rock for Choice

1. Judith Peraino, "PJ Harvey's 'Man-Size Sextet' and the Inaccessible, Inescapable Gender," *Women and Music: A Journal of Gender and Culture* 2 (1998): 47–63.

2. David Peisner, "Let It Bleed: The Oral History of PJ Harvey's 'Rid of Me,'" *SPIN*, March 31, 2015, https://www.spin.com/2013/05/pj-harvey-rid -of-me-oral-history-steve-albini/.

Chapter 6: When It Was Time for the Door to Close, It Was Shut

1. Judith M. Bennett, "The Patriarchal Equilibrium," in *History Matters: Patriarchy and the Challenge of Feminism* (Philadelphia: University of Pennsylvania Press, 2007), 54–81.

2. Ginia Bellafante, "Is Feminism Dead?," *Time*, June 29, 1998.

3. Elaine Tyler May, *Homeward Bound: American Families in the Cold War Era* (New York: Basic Books, 2017), 5.

4. Joan Wallach Scott, "The Problem of Invisibility," in *Retrieving Women's History: Changing Perceptions of the Role of Women in Politics and Society*, ed. S. Jay Kleinberg (London: Berg/Unesco, 1988), 5–29.

5. Scott, "The Problem of Invisibility."

Chapter 7: Go On, Take Everything

1. Silvia Federici, *Witches, Witch-Hunting, and Women* (Oakland, CA: PM Press, 2018).

2. Federici, *Witches*.

3. Susan Faludi, *The Terror Dream: Fear and Fantasy in Post-9/11 America* (New York: Metropolitan Books, 2007).

4. Dave Haslam, "Courtney Love in Liverpool: The Scousers Who Taught the Grunge Icon How to Rock," *Guardian*, May 25, 2020, https://www .theguardian.com/music/2020/may/25/courtney-love-in-liverpool-scousers -wild-child-how-to-rock.

5. Haslam, "Courtney Love."

6. Elizabeth Wurtzel, "Girl Trouble," *New Yorker*, June 22, 1992. https:// www.newyorker.com/magazine/1992/06/29/girl-trouble.

Chapter 8: Pimps and Hos

1. Sara Benincasa, "I Worked at Woodstock '99," Medium, August 4, 2021, https://sarajbenincasa.medium.com/i-worked-at-woodstock-99-7d8ff58f0859.

Chapter 9: We Already Have Our Lady Group

1. Mark Yarm, "'Going Out of Business Since 1988!': An Oral History of Sub Pop Records," Northwest Passage, accessed March 31, 2023, http://www .revolutioncomeandgone.com/articles/7/sub-pop-history.php.

2. Martin Scherzinger, "Music, Corporate Power, and Unending War," *Cultural Critique*, no. 60 (2005): 23–67.

3. Naomi Klein, *The Shock Doctrine: The Rise of Disaster Capitalism* (London: Penguin, 2014), 118–119.

4. Klein, *Shock Doctrine*, 119.

5. Scherzinger, "Music," 24.

6. Scherzinger, "Music," 24.

7. Scherzinger, "Music," 24.

8. Susan Faludi, *The Terror Dream: Fear and Fantasy in Post-9/11 America* (New York: Metropolitan Books, 2007), 3.

9. Stephen Dowling, "Napster Turns 20: How It Changed the Music Industry," BBC, February 24, 2022. https://www.bbc.com/culture/article/20190531-napster-turns-20-how-it-changed-the-music-industry.

10. Christian G. Appy, *Working-Class War* (Chapel Hill: University of North Carolina Press, 1993); Judith M. Bennett, "The Patriarchal Equilibrium," in *History Matters: Patriarchy and the Challenge of Feminism* (Philadelphia: University of Pennsylvania Press, 2007), 54–81; James R. Currie, *Music and the Politics of Negation* (Bloomington: Indiana University Press, 2012); Bram Dijkstra, *Evil Sisters: The Threat of Female Sexuality and the Cult of Manhood* (New York: Alfred A. Knopf, 1996); Silvia Federici, *Caliban and the Witch: Women, the Body and Primitive Accumulation* (London: Penguin, 2021); Silvia Federici, *Witches, Witch-Hunting, and Women* (Oakland, CA: PM Press, 2018); John Guillory, *Cultural Capital: The Problem of Literary Canon Formation* (Chicago: University of Chicago Press, 1993); David Harvey, *A Brief History of Neoliberalism* (Oxford, England: Oxford University Press, 2007); Edward S. Herman and Noam Chomsky, *Manufacturing Consent: The Political Economy of the Mass Media* (London: Vintage Digital, 2010); Naomi Klein, *The Shock Doctrine: The Rise of Disaster Capitalism* (London: Penguin, 2014); K. Poirot, "Domesticating the Liberated Woman: Containment Rhetorics of Second Wave Radical/Lesbian Feminism," *Women's Studies in Communication* 32 (2009): 263–292; Ellen Meiksins Wood, *Democracy Against Capitalism: Renewing Historical Materialism* (Brooklyn: Verso, 2016).

Chapter 10: "I'm a Slave for You": Women in Rock Post-9/11

1. The Breeders were dropped from Elektra Records in 2004.

2. Silvia Federici, *Caliban and the Witch: Women, the Body and Primitive Accumulation* (London: Penguin, 2021).

INDEX